ENTREPRENEURSHIP

A Behavioral Journey from Inception to the Launch of Your Business and Thereafter

DALE G. KONICEK, PH.D.

ISBN: 979-8-89079-380-5 (hardcover)
ISBN: 979-8-89079-381-2 (paperback)
ISBN: 979-8-89079-382-9 (ebook)

Jetlaunch Publishing

TABLE OF CONTENTS

AUTHOR'S NOTE

WHY I WROTE THIS BOOK

The point of writing this book is to share my experience as an entrepreneur with the reader. It is a personalized approach that should provide a sense of belonging for the reader. My goal is to provide a book that can assist and support individuals exploring the idea of entrepreneurship.

From my early work experience, I learned the value of customer service and its influence in differentiating one paperboy from another. As a paperboy, I learned the concept of risk and what it meant, especially if I could not complete my collections from customers on time. Where would the money come from to purchase my papers for next week?

The entrepreneurial experience continued in my work as a landscaper. I knew little about the concept itself, but was able to get a start by cutting grass. Through the experience of also being asked to plant trees and flowers, I had to learn about it to provide the service. This is where the research protocol idea originated, where I introduced the concept of the conduit of information. The research protocol was also applied to many other entrepreneurial experiences in my career.

For example, when I started a wealth management business, I faced numerous challenges in navigating the markets and making informed product choices. I applied the research protocol to gain a deeper understanding of business and to become knowledgeable about the world of finance. Through this effort, I acquired numerous credentials to support the brand I was developing in the financial services industry. The symbols I discuss in the book, along with the branding discussion, were direct examples of this experience as a financial services professional. In addition, having the ability to read a prospect's behavior to determine their needs and goals sharpened my skills in further understanding behavior. My time as a consultant conducting training seminars for those seeking to start a business was the beginning of my learning curve in understanding entrepreneurial behavior. The stories and examples embedded in this book are directly taken from those moments of discovery.

As a professor and a trainer, I learned a great deal about how businesses are constructed. Through the workshops and seminars that I conducted, along with personalized consulting work, the idea of the dream state was formulated. The inclusion of chaos theory to describe the market came from the many episodes of reading and researching ideas as lecture material. In this book, there is coverage of chaos theory as it pertains to a description of the Abyss.

After many years of observing what people are willing to share about their entrepreneurial experiences, a void was apparent in the books available to read for aspiring entrepreneurs. Many concentrate on a business plan orientation to the process. Some focus on a skills-based approach to becoming an entrepreneur. Although all that information can be valuable, understanding the workings of the mind and what is happening daily with individuals pursuing their dreams seemed like an approach worth considering when starting a business.

It can be said that many business opportunities are lost due to an individual's inability to cope with the inner workings of the mind. Confidence, fear, and uncertainty can become roadblocks that stifle an individual's creativity. This often leads to the individual's failure to execute the business idea, rather than it not being feasible, for example. Understanding the workings of the mind can lead to a better understanding of an individual's behavior. I refer to these as Potholes and Rationales in this book. The propensity-for-risk principle is also discussed to address the fear element in starting a business.

From all the discussions I have shared with you, this is why I wrote this book. From this book, I hope you will gain a deeper understanding of the motivation behind starting a business. I would also hope that you experience a sense of peace in knowing that your dreams are as real as anything else that comes along in the journey to becoming an entrepreneur. Identifying and absorbing what comes from our dreams is worth the effort. Whether you are a beginning entrepreneur or one who has a bit of experience behind you, this book can help fill in the cracks of why you feel the way you do from day to day. I hope you enjoy the journey you are about to experience.

INTRODUCTION

Entrepreneurship is a phenomenon that started from modest beginnings for many people. It was just a thought. It was just a hunch. Maybe it can be explained as a dream. Some people have cited a childhood fascination as the root of the idea. Other people have pointed to relatives who had a business and that influenced them to start their own business. As I have come to know it, the idea of starting a business could have come from anywhere. Yet as the years pass, living with it lingers in the mind. The idea comes to our conscious self in opportune times. The idea may even change over time. The strange thing about the changes over time is that the subconscious keeps track of the changes. It's like a storybook unraveling every time the thought arises.

The composition of the business could even take different directions. This change could be the result of a new discovery of information. Or it could be due to an infusion of technology that creates different product choices. This technological change has even influenced the process of starting a business. No longer is it necessary to have a storefront to conduct business. These changes have reshaped the core of the definition of entrepreneurship, expanding it beyond our original thoughts about it. I could also say that the changes in starting a business are beyond our imagination.

The definition of a viable entity where feasibility is measured has also changed, given the presence of the digitized world. In other words, we don't need a lot of people to get things started. Actors, consultants, and educators have started businesses as influencers who publish podcasts, books, and seminars that reach potential consumers who can be influenced to purchase various products and services. Other ideas are simply enhancements to an already existing business. The goal is to start and sell the business to someone who complements what you have developed. Now that truly is beyond the imagination of many of us who grew up in the 1950s.

However you formulate the business idea, it often comes to life. And to do anything about the idea, individuals make decisions to either move forward or continue to contemplate the thought of starting a business. Colleges and universities have become aware of this curiosity. The development of courses and seminars to meet this need has shown up all across the country. An individual can now major in entrepreneurship! It is so prevalent a subject that it can be considered a movement that has no boundaries.

There are many approaches to understanding entrepreneurialism. One approach is through the study of the business plan. The various parts of the business plan help potential entrepreneurs visualize how the business can be put together. Other approaches are more skills-based, utilizing skill assessments to determine whether someone possesses the necessary skills to be an entrepreneur. There could also be a testing component to this type of approach to build a profile of an individual's strengths and weaknesses. The final determination of this approach is whether the individual is a candidate to become an entrepreneur.

All of these approaches create the structure of the study of entrepreneurship. But there is a missing link that is rarely talked about. What is the missing link? It lies in the psychological framework of the individual transforming into an entrepreneur? For example, how did the individual come to discover the business idea? What prompted the individual to proceed with the business? What interpersonal behaviors take place that can derail an individual's pursuit of becoming an entrepreneur? What interpersonal behaviors can an individual face even after launching a business?

In this book, we will go down that path of discovery. From my experience in the field, I will share with you many ideas that were discovered through the counseling of individuals pursuing entrepreneurship. In this book, we will explore the behavioral symphony that bellows through us that few individuals want to share with the public. From the haunting of one's perceived reality of this business idea, to the actual launch of the business and thereafter, individuals experience a cadre of behaviors that play out daily.

These behaviors that are examined daily are within our inner selves. They capture the essence of why people decide to start a business, and all that can happen thereafter. We will explore those items as pieces or ingredients that formulate a consciousness of oneself and the world around us. It's what entrepreneurs live with that is rarely spoken about, as most are too afraid to admit and expose themselves openly to the public.

I can also say that the book is not a replacement for an entrepreneurship class. The material in this book concentrates on behavioral experiences. It does not act as a reference for tax law, software recommendations, organizational recommendations, or anything similar. I focus strictly on the behavioral aspects of the ledger to highlight what's often missing in entrepreneurship training programs.

This book is a legitimate account of the experience I have witnessed as a consultant and financial advisor specializing in small business entities. It is a source of knowledge that is written to help entrepreneurs understand the emotional aspects of starting a business. One thing is certain: these pages share my experiences with many who have shared their stories about starting a business. With over forty-two years of testimonies from people of many means, I deliver to you the behavioral rendition of what exists in the minds of many as they journey to be an entrepreneur. And, I will also address the aftermath of the business launch and the behaviors that can determine the longevity of the business.

We start then with our imagination. Just imagine if...

I

THE DREAM STATE

It is 3:00 a.m. I awake again with the same vision I had last night. I decide to go to the living room to do some reading. After doing so, I began to feel as though I had erased the dream from my memory. I then decide to return to sleep and get some rest for tomorrow's workday. In the morning, I wake up with the dream on my mind again. I continue to question its presence. Why am I having this dream over and over again? After breakfast, I get myself ready to go to work, wondering whether my dreams are worth considering. Why do I want to start my own business? Maybe the dream will just go away on its own. But there is no time to waste. I have to get to the place that pays the bills.

My day at the office is a typical day with my usual workload. I perform the same tasks daily. I hold the same perspective toward my work life. This is what I am supposed to be doing given my training. My daily performance at this job will shape my career. Considering any other path in my career is unimaginable. But when I go to sleep at night, I have a dream about starting a business. The excitement is such that I actually would like it to happen. Perhaps when I wake up, I will begin the process of launching the business. What would my spouse think? She will probably ask how the bills will get paid. That is a good question.

This story could have many names attached to it. Many people want more from their work life but settle for less because they fail to trust the message they receive every night. It can also come from the reality of being able to leave a full-time job with benefits. Said another way, a steady paycheck!. Your ability to face the risk of failure is also a common thought. All of these messages come from the subconscious. It has everything to do with the psychological depths of where you want to go to make a living. Yet it is a place that is only an image right now. There is no experience in doing so. Getting a grasp of starting the business is difficult to envision. We see ourselves in an image that appears and reappears throughout our dream state. This transition within the spheres of consciousness continues to take place throughout the day. Examples of those visions could be connected to a different profession. You could see yourself running a business. You could see yourself retired and enjoying the fruits of your labor. Maybe you are seeing yourself living in a different country. You could even go back in time and correct a few mistakes you wish never took place. Your dreams can be anything that your subconscious desires. In our dreams, the transition is easy. In reality, a significant amount of work needs to be completed before transitioning to self-employment.

I have often referred to this dream state as a haunting of one's perceived reality. Let's take a walk into that space for a moment to get an idea of how this dream state can occur. Imagine going to sleep and in a few hours you are in a world where there is recognition of your expertise, you are recognized as a successful professional, your family and peers respect you as a wonderful person, a good spouse and parent, and you live within a lifestyle that provides everything that satisfies you. The rush of emotions that radiate throughout the dream state motivates you to embrace all that is realized in the dream. Because you are so excited about what you experienced, you are motivated to have that dream again. The enjoyment, the uplifting feelings that are experienced throughout the night, drive you to bring back that same storyline over and over again, night after night. For some, it becomes a part of life. It's fun since all one has to do is fall asleep. After doing so, you can be anything and anybody you want to be. Perhaps you could add to the storyline every night to build an empire of sorts with many storylines attached to it. Over time, in our sleep, we begin to pick one storyline to enhance ourselves depending on the kind of day we had at work, or perhaps events that have affected our family. We can create the storyline in any image we choose with no obligation other than to continue participating through our sleep. Over time, the dream state can become a reality that is experienced outside of the sleep cycle.

To clarify what the storyline concept is and what it might look like, let me share a series of storyline moments with you. This will help convey how these moments come about and later build on where they can end up in the process of becoming an entrepreneur.

After being asleep for some time, the scene unfolds. Tonight, I see myself in the garage working with a machine to produce a product I cannot see. I am filling an order that I received last week. This is my first order, and it is so important that I deliver it on time. Suddenly, a mechanical difficulty occurs, which ends up cutting the power to the machine. Although I try to fix it, I lack the necessary skills. I start to panic because I have no solution to the problem. Perhaps I could call the manufacturer to help point me in the right direction.

After having this dream, I then woke up feeling worn out from the trauma I experienced in the dream. I'm feeling tired from the stress of not being able to fix the machine. I know that this is not real, but why do I feel as though it is?

Am I going crazy or what? I convince myself that it is only temporary and a fluke at best. But as I get up and have my breakfast, it seems a bit difficult to forget about it. I leave for work still wondering how to fix the machine. Could it be that I am suffering from a trauma I experienced years ago when I worked in a factory? I have no memory of that traumatic experience.

Upon arriving at work, I begin by completing my tasks, which include analyzing purchase orders and ensuring my company has received the correct amount of merchandise before releasing it for payment. Soon it is break time. As I stroll down to the coffee bar, I am thinking about the last purchase order reviewed and how I will resolve the discrepancy. The discrepancy I found is in the order's volume numbers since the delivery numbers do not match the purchase order. As I sit down to drink my coffee, I look out the window at the cars passing by, and my environment changes. The focus is now on a conversation with the manufacturer to resolve the machine problem in the garage. Could they refer me to a company that services the machine? Oh my gosh! What is happening to me? Will this dream stop haunting me? As I try to move away from this state of mind, I find it hard to escape the dream where I'm experiencing a machine problem. At this point, I feel violated. Like someone is inside of me, directing my thoughts without my permission. *This isn't real*, I think to myself. *Let's get out of here.*

I quickly get up and return to my office to finish the morning's workload. That afternoon, I find myself working to forget what I experienced in my dream and concentrate on the work I am paid to do. For the rest of the day, I am focused in such a way as to describe it as 'running away from this haunting perception'. I've started to notice how much time it is taking to deal with this nonsense. With a little luck, this stuff will pass. At least that is what I am telling myself.

When I get home, I have dinner with my family and enjoy a lively conversation with my spouse. I hesitate to discuss my dream with my spouse because I think she would start to worry about me. That would be the last thing I would want to do, given our very stable lifestyle with my current job. We enjoy talking about our kids and their escapades that took place during the day. After having a wonderful night of conversation with my spouse, it's time to get some sleep for tomorrow's workday.

After a few hours of sleep, I find myself submerged in the dream state. The storyline continues.

The scene unfolds as I am back talking with a repairperson who has given me the cost and time frame needed to fix the machine. Unfortunately, I will have little time to meet the deadline for my order and thus, will have to work the night to get it completed. After working through all of the problems, I complete the order and arrange to have it shipped. I meet the deadline set for the order. This accomplishment creates a feeling of exuberance I have not felt before. It was like it actually happened, and I am patting myself on the back for a job well done.

Surprisingly enough, I wake with the same feeling as if I had just accomplished something big. I am actually happy. I have a source of energy that is unusual. I normally get up feeling energetic, but this feeling is different. The strange thing about this feeling is that it's based on a circumstance that is not real. I am in a state of mind where I am celebrating an event that never happened.

I went about my routine that morning, getting dressed and having breakfast. I leave for work feeling like I am nourished and accomplished. While driving to work, it's like I awaken from this perceived reality in a different skin. As I had these thoughts, I began to realize that the car was driving itself to work. I am simply a passenger enjoying the ride in la-la land. Is this crazy or what?

After having a super productive day at work, I am back home and looking forward to watching a movie with my family. Whether my spouse notices any change in me from that awesome dream the night before, I do not know. I wonder if I am acting differently toward my family. As the movie ends and we prepare for sleep, I wonder to myself whether I will have that dream again. I tell myself I won't have that dream tonight. Maybe it will go away somehow. But then I get a sense that my subconscious does not want it to leave. For some reason, I am enjoying the thrill of being self-employed.

After falling asleep, my dream state begins to generate another storyline.

I find myself on the way to an appointment to visit with my only client. As I continue to sleep, the next scene is a conversation with the purchasing manager, who is asking me about my ability to produce more products and when delivery can be expected. Of course, I tell him what he wants to hear and commit myself to a series of larger orders. I envision what it will mean to have a company that is producing larger orders, with many employees and multiple locations, to provide for such a scenario. With that vision, I have an idea of what my lifestyle will become and how I can provide for my family. I am becoming successful overnight. Is this really possible?

As I awaken, it becomes clear to me that something is happening inside of me that is creating this dual reality for me. I start to think that maybe in a past life I owned a manufacturing company or something. I remember back in college exploring the subject of reincarnation and how people have dreams about themselves. They think they lived a life in a past time frame and reincarnated into this current space of reality. If that were the case, maybe I could have been Andrew Carnegie or Henry Ford.. After thinking about this ridiculous frame of mind, I work to gather myself and focus on paying the bills.

Throughout my workday, I am enthralled with the idea of starting a manufacturing business. Over and over again, this entrepreneur idea is at the forefront of my thinking. I begin to feel as though the dream state is taking over my conscious self to the point where I lose track of where I am and the work I am supposed to be completing. This perceived reality continues to haunt me daily. This circumstance leads me to believe that I may need some help. After reading a bit about this behavior, the condition of cognitive dissonance keeps coming up as a definition of the behavior. Let's take a look at why I have come to this conclusion.

GROWING DAYTIME DISSONANCE

As my entrepreneur vision unfolds and many episodes play out for days and months, I begin to see that what I am doing at work for this company is not satisfying me any longer. The perception has taken on its own reality. The separation between my dream state and my conscious self is razor-thin. Over time, I start to identify problems in my work and realize I need to be somewhere else. I start to become disappointed with myself because I see myself in another role in life. My current role is not fulfilling to me. The rush of being my own boss and having more freedom to do what I want becomes infectious.

Not only is the idea infectious, but the storyline begins to expand itself. Each night, a new episode is added to the reality of being self-employed. Now, the storyline is describing the reality of the small manufacturing company in different ways. From the garage scene, I expand into a larger facility that becomes a manufacturing company. I began to live in a role I didn't have. My inner behavior plays out scenes as if they are actually occurring. Every night, a new storyline is added, propelling me toward the possibility that I should focus on starting my own business instead of staying in this company and not fulfilling my potential. Will this dream state ever stop? What am I to do with all of these ideas? Should I go to see a doctor about these dreams? Maybe I am going crazy and losing my grip on reality. Perhaps I can take a pill and erase this dream state. On the other hand, I am starting to like it. I look forward to the next episode. Am I addicted or something?

That is an example of what a storyline is and how it can fester into a reality lived out daily in the mind of the individual. This is a condition called cognitive dissonance. The problem is, it is not industry-specific. It can happen to anyone who sees themselves in roles that have an opposing belief or value system. For example, why did I pick manufacturing? I could have chosen anything. In one of my consulting assignments, when I taught entrepreneurship on the road, I had one participant share with me that she had dreams of starting an organic fast food restaurant featuring watercress sandwiches. I thought she was a bit off her rocker, to be honest about it. But I was paid to help her, not criticize her. To her, it was real. It was her dream. She actually constructed the menu over time. In working with her, I would ask why add that item to the menu. She responded that she envisioned people wanting it. She saw the request for the item in her dream. She lived in that dream state for some time. She found a way to live with the opposing roles she was experiencing by packaging the dreams of her business. Cognitive dissonance was managed as a way to operate rather than a fight between roles.

I had another participant who had dreams of operating a car wash. I asked him if he had any experience with a car wash business. His response was no. I asked if he knew how a car wash works. The answer was no. I asked him why he wanted to open a car wash business. He mentioned that every day, he passed by a car wash in his neighborhood on his way to work. He also said that he notices the traffic there on the weekend. He remarked that it would be a great business to sit back and make money 24/7. In his case, he committed himself to studying the concept of a car wash. He learned about the pumps and water usage. He did all of this while working as a warehouse clerk. After studying the concept, he indicated he was prepared to make the launch. When I directed him to complete a business plan, his dream took off. Over the next year, his dream became his life. He did open a car wash. He overcame the cognitive dissonance condition. By working daily to support the feasibility of his dream, he proved that it was possible. To experience something like this example up front is to be convinced that the dream state is a powerful motivator in starting a business.

Over the years, I have had numerous sessions with individuals who were willing to share their ideas with me. The examples I have utilized here to describe how the dream state works are just that. I could have picked any of the businesses I worked with as a consultant. And actually, any business could be developed from the dream state. It's all in the imagination as to where one sees themselves. Who am I to get in the way?

The universal principles behind any storyline have to do with the new role that one sees themselves performing. It also has to do with the behavior that is generated from the idea of being a successful owner of your own business. Both go hand in hand. And no matter how much space is between the idea and reality, it has no bearing on the strength of the storyline. In other words, you do not have to have any money, or any experience, or anything that would lead to the conclusion that anything fits into the role you now want to play. Is that not a cool thing! No wonder our subconscious wants to play that storyline over and over again. Now, maybe it is clear why those who have these dreams have a hard time getting rid of them. That euphoria that is created from the storylines nightly becomes so attractive that it garners one's attention to the point of addiction.

Now, given that I have shared a glimpse of what the dream state looks like, there are other aspects of it to consider. The behavior is one aspect that can range from acceptance to avoidance. In other words, you either accept what you are thinking or you work to avoid the subject. The more concerning aspect would be the life cycle of the dream state. Imagine if this cycle extends itself to a time frame that lasts for a year or two. And although I have never heard of someone going mad or being hospitalized with mental illness, I would not be surprised that there could be a negative reaction to this dream state. And because of this haunting throughout the day, the urge to step away from the mundane existence perceived in the current work life can certainly result in a behavioral issue. Some thoughts that come to mind are depression, elusiveness, quick temper, and lack of ambition on the job, to name a few. Given that this behavioral issue could become serious, how does one cope with this haunting? The question was partially answered in the previous examples: the healthy fast food restaurant and the car wash. But let's dig a bit deeper into the topic.

Let's first start with a question. The question that is often asked is why. Why do people toil at such thoughts throughout the night? What is it about such people that drives them to enhance the story night after night? Do they suffer from a deficiency? Are they dissatisfied with their lives somehow? And since the story never ends, the library of storylines begins to be large enough to crowd out one's thinking during the day. This situation can cause one to lose track of reality. This is the beginning of the haunting of one's perceived reality? It's considered a haunting because it continues to interfere with not only sleep cycles but also everyday life. One begins to live a life that is merely a perception. That perception reinforces the idea that your current situation in both your work and family life is no longer acceptable. Left alone to fester, it could result in erratic behavior toward others and family members. Although the actual intent is not to commit to such behaviors, the imaginative world is no longer distinguishable from reality. This then leads to behavior that would not usually take place daily. Although the situation I present may be perceived as an extreme case of cognitive dissonance, other levels of dissonance also exist. It could occur in stages where the severity of the behavior builds over time. One thing is for sure: it's a real behavior that has been shared with me by numerous people. Counseling has been suggested to address the behavior. I think an understanding of the new profile would be a start to addressing the behavior you exhibit toward your surroundings.

UNDERSTANDING THE NEW PROFILE

To understand and interpret the feelings generated by our dream state condition, a breakdown of the storyline concept can help answer why it occurs so frequently. The first major realization is that the storyline was not picked consciously. So, who or what is driving the storyline? Where are these thoughts coming from? And if I want to erase these thoughts from my mind, how do I do that? Realize that those thoughts are there because you are putting them out in front of your conscious self. This action is to remind you of past references to the subject or storyline at hand. Although you may not remember exactly where the idea originated, somewhere in your past, it hit you in such a way as to drill itself into your subconscious. So, you are not crazy, and you are not alone in having vivid dreams of how you see yourself.

So, how can I escape from this cycle? Or better yet, do you actually want to stop having these dreams? The pleasure received from these dreams can become addictive. The sensation received from the dream state creates the struggle of breaking out of it. Suppressing or terminating the dream state may be remedied by taking sleep aids or visiting a doctor. Surely, my logical self is supporting the other side of the struggle. Concentrate on what your current reality provides for you (e.g., the comfort of having a paycheck coming in with health care and a stable environment for my family). That may be reason enough to create the motivation to silence the haunting. No one but you can decide to proceed or to attempt to erase what is clearly in your mind as your self-portrait.

So, whether you accept the role you want to play in life or resolve the issue by suppressing it, an action must take place to remedy the situation. There is yet a third solution, and that is to continue to live out both lives, hoping to find a way to make the transition. I have heard stories from those who did not make the transition. They often talk about wanting to start their own business, but never take the time or energy to make it happen. Some people respond that they plan to start a business upon retirement. I urge you to think about that idea before deciding whether to move forward or wait until you retire to repeat the same verse. By the time you retire, so many things have the possibility of changing. Will the business idea you have today still be a valid business idea later on in retirement?

This question reminds me of stories I have collected over the years about waiting until retirement to start the business. I had a number of individuals who I counseled in my outplacement work who were near retirement or at retirement. A few people shared their thoughts with me about starting a business. The common denominator among these individuals is whether they had the energy to actually launch a business. Were they willing to now take the risk with retirement capital to start a business?

Was their health at a point where physical activity is a problem? Due to these variables, many who initially considered waiting until retirement altered the storyline in their dream state to focus on tinkering with something. For example, I counseled a gentleman who had two Ph.D.s. He had worked in the oil and gas business as a scientist. When he came to me, he wanted to start a furniture manufacturing business. He indicated that he was very good at building furniture and had thoughts of starting a business. After I asked him some typical questions regarding space and investment requirements, he decided to move forward with the idea. After conducting the research and considering his options, his dream state changed. His original idea of opening up a small furniture-making business was gone. No longer was it feasible, given the technology available now for making furniture. He ended up working from his garage, making small pieces of furniture and wooden pen sets. In other words, it became a hobby rather than a business. Shortly thereafter, he struggled to fulfill even small orders. It was a great idea, but staying in the dream state or erasing it altogether might have had a better ending.

Examining the role that you perceive yourself fulfilling requires some self-analysis. Searching for information that qualifies the dream state vision is critical to distinguishing it from fantasy or unrealistic elements. At least now you have that in your hands to address that image in your dream state. By disqualifying it as a possibility, its composition transforms into a fantasy that is more easily dismissed in the dream state.

One variable that is a powerful tool toward the start of a business is the risk demon. It stands out as one of the most powerful eliminators of business ideas. It may, in itself, help alleviate the haunting of the dream state for those who are trying to do so. For those who want to go forward with the business idea, it is a crossroad that is challenging and unforgiving.

THE RISK DEMON

To understand this struggle between realities further, one must consider a behavior within us that applies to situations in our lives related to risk. The propensity-for-risk principle is used when considering the launch of a business. It is also prevalent in investment situations where there could be a loss of principal (cash). This loss could set you back for years. Think about the past stock market crashes. Due to the significant losses some people incurred, many never reinvested in the stock market. This fearful behavior influenced many people to avoid it. This action had an adverse effect on the ability to accumulate wealth. Do you have the capacity to take on that risk now in starting a business? This principle alone could be instrumental in whether to move forward or to bury your business idea. For those who choose to bury the idea, a rationale not to move forward will be created, whether it is valid or not. The behavior is an outgrowth of the escape plan to move away from the haunting to a place that satisfies its removal. The inability to assume risk is not new. It is a major pitfall for those seeking to become entrepreneurs. If you lack the stomach for risk, you cannot pretend it doesn't exist. Your true feelings about risk are valid and should be respected. Remember, you may imagine yourself as an entrepreneur, but it does not mean you are one. And, do not pretend that you can overcome your low propensity for risk by simply forcing the transition from employee to owner. Worry and fear are behaviors that can create major health problems and numerous other problems that are difficult to unravel once they occur. It is better to either eliminate the business idea or learn to cope with the various risks that you will face throughout your time as an entrepreneur. Let's then move on to face the realities that arise from the vision of transitioning into an entrepreneur.

Examining the Vision toward Reality

If I were to tell you that managing this haunting behavior is part of the process of converting oneself to being an entrepreneur, you might not believe me. But every entrepreneur I have come across has carefully provided information that connects to what I have just shared with you. The haunting that they experience is held tight under the chest, so to speak, because it does not sell well to the public surrounding them. Imagine telling someone that your dreams of starting a business are haunting you? The public's perception of you may take a different direction than what was planned. The public generally thinks that a business idea is developed through more of a technical process rather than a behavioral vision. But, when examining a company's vision statement, could it not have come from an individual's dream state? After all, why is it called a vision statement? Where did the vision come from?

The dreams and storylines that are written within the mind are where all reality comes from when it comes to entrepreneurship. One does not think in a void where references and life experiences are erased easily, nor do they come from some clean slate of consciousness that produces ideas that generate products and services for commercial development. Our visions of ourselves and our businesses are built over time in storylines that come from the subconscious. Yet, who would admit that what they are constructing is from a storyline they have built over the last month or so in their sleep. Perhaps one can even contemplate years in the making. Over the years, entrepreneurs have testified that many of their current endeavors originated from ideas that surfaced in the past, not the present. Again, few will admit that they saw themselves in a dream.

These storylines haunt many individuals, and many do nothing about them. For whatever reason, they live within a reality that never comes to the surface. Something does not happen. And yet imagine how these individuals walk around every day with the storylines battering their conscious selves. Scary!!

The haunting of your perceived reality is not a fluke. It is a reality that has its roots in something that drives you to that place. And whether you want to go there or not, your subconscious state takes you there to reinforce your direction in life. If this haunting does not take place, and if the storylines never take place, it is in this bifurcation that separates entrepreneurs from blue-collar owners. Without a place where vision and innovation generate themselves, one will be like punching a clock and reporting to work to implement a sterile set of task structures. Over time, this will dissipate because nothing fuels the production of vision and innovativeness. Without a source for ideas, the only thing left is one's sweat, which evaporates over time. There are exceptions, though, to every rule. Some people work to live, with no ambition to be self-sufficient. Their approach to extracting ideas involves copying or benchmarking what their competitors produce. Those businesses become more of a lifestyle entity where everything is managed based on how it fits into the owner's lifestyle. Given what we have learned about entrepreneurs, it would be difficult to refer to these individuals as entrepreneurs. They are often referred to as cookie cutters or copycats. In other words, they copy from their competitors. Frequently, the competitor is a large company. The process of differentiation then breaks down since there is nothing in the tank to help create or innovate. It often comes down to a price war. Guess who often wins? There is no magic in the number of businesses that fail in the first five years of existence. The lack of vision and its ability to create and innovate are key to survival. Our dream state is a great place where things begin, whether we want to accept it or not.

There comes a day when one gets tired of the fight. The struggle becomes worrisome, and action becomes a front-and-center activity. But how does one go about transitioning to the other side of the ledger? How does one decipher the tea leaves in the storylines experienced daily? What do I do with my behavior in the meantime while I figure all this out? In this next part, I will unravel that situation and answer all those questions. I will also give a pathway to that perceived reality that is waiting to be realized.

Takeaways from Part I: The Dream State

- Dreams are real and should be respected as a source of information
- The dream state can act as a motivating force toward starting a business
- Conflicting roles can lead to cognitive dissonance, which can lead to negative behaviors
- Cognitive dissonance can be addressed through a research-oriented approach to qualifying the dream (Business idea).
- A research-oriented approach to understanding a business idea (dream) can be a useful tool in either accepting or rejecting the dream state (Business idea)
- The propensity-for-risk principle is a powerful tool that can be used to determine the feasibility of becoming an entrepreneur.
- Differentiating yourself from others is achieved through vision. Vision is realized through the creative and innovative properties of the mind (your vision or dream state).

II

THE TRANSITION

If you are trying to figure out how to help an individual trapped in a dream of starting a business but struggling to make it a reality, let's be clear about this major revelation. Not everyone is cut out to be an entrepreneur, even if they imagine themselves as one. A good starting point for this discovery period is to explore standard methods used to assess the feasibility of the transition. One strategy that could be helpful is first to review the determinants that shape the environments and specific skill sets of those who have made the transition. Let's start with the behavioral determinants.

BEHAVIORAL DETERMINANTS

Regardless of the profession a person is currently in, entrepreneurs often emerge from all of them. I have witnessed situations where individuals with mechanical ability, like auto techs, open up auto repair shops that flourish for years. Individuals working in the trades professions, such as carpenters, welders, electricians, and HVAC workers, often decide to break away from larger organizations and start private enterprises that become successful at providing personal service to the community at large. Generally, many start businesses that are directly related to the work they currently perform for an employer. I have also witnessed highly professional people start businesses in their respective professions. Examples of these professions would be accountants, attorneys, and financial advisors. Many have opened up private practices and grown into family practices with numerous associates operating together under one brand.

I have also witnessed both groups venture out into unrelated fields to start businesses. Many franchisees who have started fast food restaurants, for example, did not have prior experience in the fast food industry. A prime example is with McDonald's franchise owners. Many who bought franchises had managerial and administrative capabilities that helped build knowledge of operating a fast food restaurant. McDonald's helped with formal training and guidance to support the successful operation of the franchise. Many franchisee owners were part of a company environment, working as managers or administrators in unrelated industries. They can manage and learn, providing an opportunity to cross over into an unfamiliar area of expertise. To be realistic, though, other professional types have difficulty with the idea of starting a business.

Over the years, I have witnessed a pattern of behavior by certain professionals that often leads to a more conservative perspective of work. In other words, they struggle to transition from employee to owner. This does not mean that all do not succeed in making the transition. It simply means they tend to either shun the situation altogether or take more time to complete the transition. Let me give an example of what I have experienced.

How often do we see that even smart people, who are geniuses at what they do, struggle to start a business? The major problems found among this group of people have to do with four distinct behavioral types. The first type involves individuals who struggle with the role change. They simply do not see themselves operating in the role of an owner. The second type of behavior relates to the difficulty in determining how to start a business based on the work already performed daily for an employer. The third type involves individuals who struggle to transition between industries. Often, the capital requirements necessary to enter the business become a deterrent in the transition. The business they currently work for as an employee incurs huge financial costs to become a competitor. These professionals allow this hurdle to be a deterrent to their transition. When looking at other industries for possible opportunities, they often struggle to visualize the possibilities. The rationalization that it's too difficult to achieve the transition shapes their behavior going forward. The fourth type is associated with individuals who struggle to manage risk. The idea that a paycheck will not be coming every two weeks is motivation enough to avoid the entrepreneur mindset.

Examples of professionals who exhibit these types of behaviors are as follows: scientists, computer analysts, and teachers. This list is not exhaustive, but clarifying why they exhibit any of the four behaviors listed will help in understanding the inability to transition. Often, these professionals excel in their areas of training, but struggle to apply that knowledge to their own businesses. Many have had innovative ideas while working for their employer that have led to a new business opportunity. That circumstance does not make them entrepreneurs. In addition, the personality of some individuals does not warrant a journey into self-employment. Some individuals are followers, not leaders. This is why they do not see themselves as owners. Some people are more introverted, which drives them to professions that have little contact with the public. In addition, they tend to dislike the process of selling themselves to others. And, more importantly, some are just not risk takers and thus will not take chances in disturbing their safety net.

Along with the behavioral determinants, other factors have a profound influence on choosing the role of entrepreneur. These determinants are sometimes invisible to the individual who they influence. Let's take a look at the environmental determinants that are central to an individual's understanding of the business world.

ENVIRONMENTAL DETERMINANTS

Regardless of whether I examine an individual in the trades or professional occupations, the environmental factors that are experienced as employees have common elements that become references. These references are utilized when analyzing business situations and opportunities. But do those experiences transfer to an entrepreneurial environment? Let's examine what those references are in the corporate environment.

The corporate environment is a closed architecture, meaning it already has many of the elements needed to construct a new business. Funding for the latest business opportunity or situation is provided through a departmental budget. The company offers additional expertise and human resources. Paychecks arrive every other week regardless of the progress of the business opportunity. And when it's time to take vacation time, it's no problem leaving the workplace since other employees are there to continue the work. That scenario is not what entrepreneurs' experience. Those individuals assigned to projects may think that they are running a business because of the autonomy given by management to make decisions. But let's be clear, those employees operate in a structure that is departmentalized, with many resources at their disposal. There is no risk of capital that the individual will experience. And all the services provided by the company support the process of acting like a business. This used to be called intra-preneurialism. There is no substitute for entrepreneurship, no matter what it's called. Entrepreneurs have to create everything in the structure and are at risk for the results of that work. Understanding these environmental determinants and applying the knowledge helps clarify how our environmental experience influences our current thinking. In other words, where does all of what I know come from? Knowing and understanding the origin of your thought processes is paramount to constructing your island of opportunities. If a person's entire background is in a corporate environment, it will be necessary to create a pathway to the knowledge required to start a business.

YOUR NEW REALITY

I think we can agree that working for a company where every element of the business is positioned or available without risk to the individual creates a reality that has little to do with what entrepreneurs experience. It thus shapes the thinking of the individual. So now, what if those environmental experiences that you bring to the arena are not pertinent to this new environment you are creating? For example, what if one had to construct a mission statement? How about finding a place to conduct business? (i.e., office building or factory)? What about hiring people and constructing a compensation and benefits system? Who will be your legal counsel? You see, all of that was already in place for you when working for an employer. I could certainly discuss the marketing and departmental budgets and revenue creation further, but I think the point has been made. The transference of expertise that prepares you to launch a business outside of the company you currently work for has little correlation to being pertinent to operating your own business. As an owner, the environments are different; the mindset in decision-making is on a different platform, given the difference in its access to financial resources. Let's also add that your personal assets can be at risk, which significantly alters the perspective newcomers have when transitioning.

What many dreamers take for granted is that everything in their dream is already in place. All aspects of the organization are operating to generate business. Stepping into the reality of being an entrepreneur, there will be nothing in place for you regarding organizational and operational structures, human resources, or financial resources. It will be like a blank sheet of paper, ready for you to create structures that communicate and produce a product or service. That structure will generate revenue to cover expenses and build a brand that has a life of its own. I have often referred to this mark as your Mona Lisa. It will indeed be your creation. Do you see yourself weathering this challenge? Regardless of whether you do or not, one thing that must take place is to visualize your dream. To accept or reject the idea, you will need to know its composition. You can start by visualizing the dream.

VISUALIZING THE DREAM

Now that we have examined the behavioral and environmental determinants that help quantify what the transition may look like, let's dig a bit deeper into your vision. From the start of this haunting, you have been visualizing what this business is without formulating the specifics. In other words, since you were not starting a business and had made no commitments to it, why not just keep dreaming? It may be because you have the motivation to make it a reality. So, what does that reality look like? Well, let's visualize it. First, let's go back to the storyline of the person who sees themselves as a manufacturer. This visualizing exercise may take some time to formulate, but it's worth the effort. Let's ask some questions:

- In your dream, what industry do you work in?
- Does your storyline advance itself to having multiple facility locations?
- Is your vision in a virtual environment?
- In the work that you currently perform, is there a transfer of skill sets between roles?
- Have you ascertained why your subconscious chose the industry that you chose to operate in?
- How does the customer utilize your product or service
- Does your product have commercial use or residential use? Or does it serve both markets?
- Does your idea need infrastructure? Employees?
- How much money would you need to start the business?

There would be a lot of information that could come from such an exercise. And whether I chose manufacturing or any other industry, the same questions would be similar. The key is the ability to integrate in a way that creates a sense of how things connect. How do you operationalize functions within an organizational entity that deliver a product or service to the public?

I believe this method of discovery is more effective in determining an individual's potential for success in building a sustainable business than a skills inventory approach. It is this rudimentary knowledge that often gets lost when focusing solely on a skills inventory approach. The process of visualizing them can provide the gateway to exploring the business model and product or service offerings that are actually attainable. It can also build a model that constructs a series of interactions to build the knowledge needed for the transition. That is what I was referring to when I mentioned that a pathway to transition may be needed for those lacking experience or perspective for the business startup.

To help with this pathway concept, an individual can utilize the dream state to gain further knowledge about the business. The visualization process during the dream state can continue to happen while moving through this transition. During that period, there are moments when an individual will wake up during the night with ideas relating to the business.. Since most people experience this while waking up during the night, it would be helpful to record whatever you have envisioned throughout the night. For those business owners who will admit to having dreams about their businesses, many have shared with me the idea of keeping a pad of paper and a pencil on the nightstand when they awaken during the night. This can happen before, during, and after the launch. Writing down ideas can help you recall them later. In this case, though, you are not looking to relive the idea of being a business owner, but in how you will operate as one. This attitude and perspective will lead to further identifying and solidifying the business idea.

SOLIDIFYING THE IDEA

In my entrepreneurship classes and seminars that I have con- ducted over the years, one exercise that is essential to the discovery period is what I refer to as the behavioral quiz. After the visualization exercise, a good way to record what is seen is to write it down in a format that is useful to your launch. This questioning process is an examination and a preparation of one's belief system that tests whether an individual is ready for the world of entrepreneurship. In other words, it helps solidify your ideas. It also tests the individual's knowledge of the business they are about to launch. The examination is in the form of a series of open-ended questions that challenge students and participants to verbalize their visions of the business they are about to launch. The process it creates is also different for each student and participant, since its mean- ing incorporates different behavioral episodes experienced throughout a person's life. This includes work experience and the roles that were played while employed in a profession. Every individual who participates in answering the questions can get clarity on what they know or don't know. This clarity can help determine whether it's time to throw in the towel and go back to the dream state, or continue formulating plans to launch the business. On the other hand, it could also encourage the decision to find a rationale to eliminate the idea by suppressing and eliminating the haunting. Whatever it may bring, the process can move you to some conclusion.

The following are the questions that are typical of the behavioral exercise:

Question Number 1

- What in your work life did you do that would warrant the skills needed to operate a business?

Would this question not make you think about whether your dreams are real or not? Would it not force you to think about yourself, not superfluously, or in the dream state, but to analyze your background to search for whatever it is you have in your skill set that transfers to the world of entrepreneurship? And notice that the question does not address a specific business. It simply asks whether you have the skills to operate a business.

Question Number II

- Why would someone hire you?

Given that consumers have a choice, what is it about you that stands out among the possible choices consumers have when considering the product or service you are offering?

Said in another way, if you were the customer, what would have to happen conceptually to decide on whether to hire someone like yourself? What is a critical skill or knowledge base that you possess that would be instrumental in helping your customer decide on doing business with you?

This question serves a dual purpose, as it can also be used as a job interview question. Rather than it being the business that you want someone to embrace, it may be that you have now decided to pursue a different job opportunity. So, preparing to answer the question is helpful if you choose not to start a business and will now seek a new job opportunity. It can also help you sell yourself to an employer when a promotion or salary raise is a target opportunity. Regardless of where this knowledge is utilized, it is a benefit no matter where you are headed.

Questions Number III–V

- What differentiates your business offerings from your competitors?
- How are you different from everyone else in the market?
- What makes you unique?

It's time to prepare for the market competition you'll face during your launch. When making the effort to answer these questions reasonably, the one element that needs to be present is what everyone in your industry is doing. Perhaps that was not in your dream! It's usually missing because, remember, there is often more euphoria than work in the dream state. Answering this question requires knowledge of your industry. Are you currently working in the industry where you want to open your own business? If not, how will you know how to compete in that industry with the knowledge necessary to differentiate yourself from everyone else? How will you design the marketing effort or write the marketing plan in your business plan if you do not know who you compete against? For instance, when delivering a sales presentation to a group of buyers, it is not unusual for them to have questions. One question that is often asked is: "How are you different from...." The name of the company competing with you may very well be who the buyer is referring to. I can confidently say that if you don't know who your competition is, how can you differentiate yourself from the competition you don't recognize or understand? That situation would be one embarrassing moment and probably the end of your presentation.

The other two questions are there because your business model may be different in such a way that not only is the product distinct, but the way that you plan to conduct business is also different. One example of this is the company Top Golf. Driving ranges have been around for a long time. They are simply nets, grass, lighting, and yardage signs. Top Golf reinvented the idea with food, drinks, games, and opportunities for group entertainment events, along with nets, lighting, and yard signage. Forget the grass! Now that's what I call a different way of doing business. So, these other two questions are there so that you have a chance to verbalize those differences in organizational format, business models, or in a unique marketing ploy that is applied to the industry, like Top Golf.

Few people I have met have a complete profile of their businesses, which is necessary to answer all these questions thoroughly. It does help to move the individual along, though, in the process of their transition from dream state to the transition state. Either direction would be considered progress in figuring out whether you feel fit to be an entrepreneur or not. It can also be a barometer for whether or not you are ready to become an entrepreneur. In other words, you may have the ingredients to become an entrepreneur, but lack the confidence to move forward toward the transition state. The lack of knowledge and understanding of the entrepreneurial role is a major setback for many who want to be entrepreneurs.

Now that we have taken the behavioral test, how do your dreams look now? Do you feel the same way about them that you now feel after taking the quiz? Is the transition closer than you initially thought? Or are you feeling like you have been hit by a train? Either way, you are making progress.

Now, let's move on to help fill in the areas where knowledge is needed. This provides another clear pathway to the transition. In many cases, the product or service individuals aim to provide remains unknown because the dream state is not designed to be specific. To get specific, we need more fuel in the tank. That fuel is related to additional resources. More information that helps make decisions is called the conduit-of-information concept.

THE CONDUIT OF INFORMATION

Most often, new business owners do not answer questions about which product to align themselves with. They address which products and services to consider by sector or industry, given that most available information is formulated to address industry and sector opportunities. The reason for this form of information is that most economic research and forecasting information utilizes government and research organizations that conduct sector analysis as a basis for the interpretation of business activity and business opportunities.

For example, investors will identify sectors that are attractive given the growth opportunities discovered through a research process. An example would be the technology sector. If a business owner wants to identify a hot opportunity in technology, the same answers that investors receive from forecasting reports are the same information utilized to determine business opportunities. This process compels you to develop a research protocol to gather and analyze market information that aligns with your business. This process is known as placing your hand on the conduit-of–information. This process leads to business competence. You will then know that what you envision in your sleep is actually something that can be viewed in your conscious state. When that happens, this opens the door for further inquiry. One tool often used to extract information from the marketplace is the networking tool. The networking tool is part of the conduit-of-information concept.

THE NETWORKING TOOL

To gain a deeper understanding of the conduit of information, you have the option to speak directly to entrepreneurs. There is no better resource to utilize than the actual people who are doing what you envision yourself doing in the future. What if you could talk to someone who is, for example, a manufacturer? What if you could find a way to learn about the business that you envision yourself performing before becoming totally committed to making a launch? Would there be a way to work for someone in the industry first before launching your business? This step would help test your vision before committing resources to the startup process. Working in the field where your startup is headed will go a long way toward formulating more concrete ideas about your potential business. In other words, you will see what your competitors are doing and develop a plan to compete with them! Networks share information through meetings and social events. It is the attendance at these events that can create a conduit of information for you. The information will be current and relevant, given that it's derived from current market activity. Another place that generates useful information is through educational programs. Acquiring fundamental knowledge of key areas can prepare you to construct the business plan.

Specific areas that are commonly influenced within the business plan are the organizational, operational and marketing plans.

EDUCATIONAL PROGRAMS

Other opportunities that may help make your transition from the dream state to the reality of starting a business are through entrepreneurship programs. There is coursework at colleges and universities that covers the subject of entrepreneurship.. Some courses address the various operations within a business plan. Some training programs begin by administering skills inventories and Myers-Briggs tests to categorize an individual's skill set and behavioral profiles. This helps identify the roles and environments that may be a better fit for an individual based on the results. There are also degree programs that cover many business functions that are incorporated in a business operation. For example, accounting, finance, and management courses are included in the degree program to create a foundation of understanding of what entrepreneurs face in operating their businesses. All of these programs help individuals write business plans, which record one's vision within a series of plans that lay out what the business is and how it will operate. This is a worthy effort but it cannot be effective if it overlooks the behavioral process of qualifying the business as being a sustainable business. The visualization and behavioral question process described previously tends to help aspiring entrepreneurs much more than putting a business plan together that lacks substance to plan with or execute.

There is another tool that can be just as useful as all the options I have covered up to this point. Now, let's take another look at risk and how it can be utilized as a tool for information.

PROPENSITY-FOR-RISK REVISITED

After visualizing and answering questions about your vision, along with the research protocol and coursework that help formulate your business launch plan, it seems to me that other questions need to be asked. These questions would complement what was discovered in the answers to the behavioral exercise questions discussed earlier. Building on that knowledge through further inquiry may give more meaning to you.

Risk aversion is probably the number one reason why people decide to sleep on the topic of starting a business. This concept is also called the propensity-for-risk principle when it is directed at an individual. It serves as a powerful deterrent to transitioning from the dream state to launching your business. Because so many individuals have been coddled through corporate environments, they have had little experience in dealing with risk. I refer back to my examples of corporate environments where there is an existing structure with a multitude of services available at your disposal.. But one of the main determinants in becoming an entrepreneur is the ability to take risks with your own capital. Because of the corporate experience that many are subject to, few are exposed to actually risking personal capital. So when the time comes to start a business where capital is at risk, alarms go off in the minds of those who do not have the experience of accepting a margin of risk. The only experience that may be present is when individuals invest their own capital in the purchase of a stock or mutual fund. This experience often occurs when investing in a corporate retirement plan or an individual investment program. But, this is not the same as risking your working capital, meaning your salary or your life's savings.

I mention the propensity-of-risk principle again, as it applies throughout the process between the dream state and the reality of the launch. And since you may have a better idea about how your business will operate, the risk aversion test may address those new discoveries in your business idea that change how you will operate now, rather than in the dream state. To strengthen that concept, let's take another quiz that I have presented to my Entrepreneurship classes that helps address the proponents of risk in a startup.

QUESTIONS TO ASSESS RISK

- How is revenue created?
- How long is the business cycle?
- You are looking at your monthly revenue and discover that payroll cannot be covered for both you and your employees. Would you be okay with not paying yourself?
- What measures would you have in place if revenues did not cover your monthly expenses?
- Could you cope with the idea that you may have to budget your household expenses to conform to the erratic stream of income you receive from the business?
- What runs through your mind when you secure a loan that amounts to more than all the assets you currently own?
- What does the daily work schedule look like?
- It's Monday morning, the first day away from the corporate environment. What are you doing this morning? What are your plans for today?
- Who do you plan on meeting with this week? What will be the purpose of that meeting?
- Who are your competitors, and what type of competitive environments are created when competing with them?

These questions are designed to be somewhat repetitive to get different views of the target subject matter. Answers to these questions will then help to formulate marketing plans and differentiating strategies for your business. There is yet another aspect to this line of questioning that sends a powerful message to the individual. That message has to do with the structure of your working life.

In corporate America, you had a job description. In contrast, as a business owner, there is no job description. So, organizing one's work life is quite different between environments. Perhaps we should thank the organizations you have worked for in the past, as they have provided you with a structured life. For example, you were told when to start work, end work, go to lunch, go on break, and perhaps when to retire. What a service! Now all of that is up to you. Do you actually think you will create the same structure? And this is where the risk is prevalent, where there is an inability to organize well enough to generate enough income to operate the business. Are you ready for that challenge?

Based on this line of questioning and line of reasoning, do you see the difference between a skills-based approach and a behavioral approach to your startup? I think both are necessary, but my opinion would support a behavioral approach first, before building a business plan. With all of this information flow, there comes a time when the question of feasibility should be addressed. In other words, with all of the information you have collected and absorbed, you are now ready to answer the big one. Is it feasible to start this business?

FEASIBILITY OF YOUR VISION

Many business courses talk about the feasibility of an idea. How does one achieve feasibility? It's not through dreaming! And believe it or not, some continue to remain in the dream state because after touching the conduit of information, they discover that the risks and workload necessary to achieve the elements of the storyline are too much to handle. And in many cases, the workload and risks identified exceed their anticipated levels. This happens a lot. This action immediately turns the individual back into a dreamer and away from the title of entrepreneur. The one element that is missing is fuel! They lack ambition and may not have a realistic outlook on who they want to be.

The idea of feasibility is constructed through the discovery of information pertinent to your vision. The collected data should lead to a conclusion about whether there is an opportunity for your vision in the market. Many entrepreneurs utilize supply and demand data to identify markets underserved by the business community. Is there a reason why it's underserved? Your vision may not be widely recognized in the business community. Does that mean it's not feasible? Or perhaps no one thought about it before. Many innovations within the technology sector were far-out ideas that many predicted would not make it. The personal computer is one. There were those who thought it was ridiculous to believe that people would want these machines. The apps market is yet another example. Who would use these apps? Most are tools that pertain to very small task structures, yet the market is booming with choices. What about the creator market? These are people who are considered influencers. They create a footprint in the social media market that influences others to purchase the products and services that sponsor their programming.

Some of the top influencers in 2025 are: Jimmy Donalson (Mr Beast), Dwayne "The Rock" Johnson, Charli D'Amelio, Darren Watkins (IShowSpeed), and Kylie Jenner. Who would have thought that this type of business would flourish into such a large business sector? The podcast business is another that comes to mind. Some of the top names are the *Mel Robbins Report*, *The Joe Rogan Experience*, *Mick Unplugged*, and *On Purpose* with Jay Shetty. These have become brand names that deliver content to the community. Advertisements for various products and services are part of the programming that supports their shows. All of these businesses were far-out technology ideas that did not have storefronts or traditional product offerings. Yet it was someone's dream that created such companies.

And to go back in time, McDonald's was an idea many did not think would make it. Who would want to eat a burger in the morning? At that time, McDonald's was a 24-hour-a-day restaurant. And who would want to eat fast food? This is what some consumers said. That did not stop Ray Kroc from educating the community on the quality of fast food and the convenience it brings to our lives.

Another direction in applying this idea of feasibility is in looking at who provides the product or service idea you have, and what is missing from those providers? What do people want but cannot get from a product or service mix? Filling in the gap with a product offering or rearranging how service is provided may be aligned with your vision. Finding a gap in the market may very well be just what your vision offers. When this is found, the strength behind determining feasibility will increase substantially.

No one can tell you when the match is perfect. The match being that your level of feasibility is enough to forecast the success of the business perfectly. There are few entrepreneurs who have ever experienced such a phenomenon. However, by staying in this discovery mode, addressing all that is created through one's behavior and findings, and being true to oneself, a workable model can be developed that is good enough to move forward with one's vision.

Other factors can hinder your progress throughout the launch process. These are those little things that become obstacles over time. It is the individual who transforms these items into obstacles. This is why you need to learn about the rationales, potholes, and fantasies that exist in the process of starting a business.

RATIONALES, POTHOLES, AND FANTASIES

Many ideas come along that can blind an upcoming entrepreneur's vision. I consider the following ideas a waste of time and energy. So why mention them? The answer has to do with the idea that entrepreneurship is a market. And you will be the target of that marketing. Like any other market, it has competitors that are selling products and services to aspiring entrepreneurs. The marketing strategies employed by some entrepreneurial businesses often sensationalize the startup process, relying on either rational or fantastical claims. This section addresses these issues and includes a few ideas on how to avoid potholes during your startup process. By avoiding these items, there may be a better chance of eliminating bad fortune in your startup. This may place you in a better state of mind to make the launch. Experiencing negativity early in the launch can be a significant determinant in not moving forward. So doubt can be a deterrent to assessing your worthiness to be an entrepreneur. Get rid of it now!

EXPERIENCE AS A RATIONALE

So let's address the idea of having experience in the industry versus someone who does not. It's one thing to get a job to learn how to do something with the thought of using it as a platform for a startup, versus someone who made a career in that same industry. Going back to the manufacturing example, if one is in a position to have manufacturing experience and has a reasonable foundation of knowledge of how the industry works, one might think that individual has a better chance at succeeding than someone who has a blank slate on the topic. Well, that is not necessarily true.

Do you recall the discussion I shared earlier about where people typically find their business references? To revisit that idea is to stress the role that individuals play in corporate settings. Reinforcing the ideas surrounding risk and the closed architecture leads to a finite set of references that are drawn from corporate platforms, not entrepreneurial scenarios. That transition to entrepreneurship based solely on corporate experience is not a given. In other words, the experience gained in a large corporate environment, where resources are readily available from the outset, does not necessarily translate directly to a startup organization. Given that your startup will have limited resources, your considerable corporate experience will not be helpful in the learning process. If you think that your lack of experience means you have no chance of starting a business in your chosen industry, discard that rationale. Do not let that idea hold you back. Many entrepreneurs are working in industries that were not planned during their college years or at any other point in their lives. Yet they became successful entrepreneurs. Then there are those dreams that are constructed to infuse the idea that starting a business is my destiny.

DESTINY AS A RATIONALE

Some individuals believe it is their destiny to start a business. Some might even argue that God ordains it for an individual to create a business to deliver a service to the masses. Although I am not closed to the idea that this could be true, it does not alleviate the process of discovery that I have discussed in this part of the book. If a person feels compelled to accept this rationale, my advice to them would be to pray for the strength to work through the process of discovery to formulate the foundation of the business.

Using the rationale of destiny by itself to support the idea that the business has feasibility is short-sighted and lacks substance. Because of the presence of this rationale, an urgency to start the business may lead to poor decision-making. Shortcuts begin to become reality.

Another aspect of this rationale has to do with an unsettled experience. This unsettled matter is the fuel behind the urgency to start the business. This urgency arises because something that should have occurred in the past did not happen. Since no action has been taken to alleviate the desire to start a business, individuals believe they must act now before it's too late. Age is a decisive factor in this thinking. Failure to start the business can be a source of this urgency. It could also come from a failed business that was started some years ago, and the individual wants another opportunity to make it happen. These sources of urgency should be avoided if possible. There is no quick route to the start of a business, regardless of the reasons for the urgency. So, forget about the destiny idea. It is not an idea that is helpful for the start of a business. One rationale, though, that could be an outgrowth of the destiny rationale is the rationale of overconfidence. This is especially true of those who are resurrecting an old business that failed. Individuals can make poor decisions when they are overconfident about themselves. They believe their skill set allows them to start the business now, eliminating the need to educate themselves on all the necessary elements to assess feasibility. People who believe in the concept of destiny often are overconfident about themselves. This is especially true of those resurrecting an old business that failed. They often feel they know what went wrong and they can fix it. As time has passed, much has changed, and thus, the business idea is not the same as it was back then. This overconfident behavior leads to avoidable startup failures. One skill that is necessary in making a successful launch is the art of listening.

Having counselors assist in the making of your business is a requirement, not a nuisance. Overconfident individuals often avoid input from others, believing they already know how to start the business. Any outside input may be perceived as interference with the progress of starting the business. Not a positive place to be.

Another aspect of this overconfidence behavior is the thought that one imagines themselves to be what the vision has provided, with nothing to support what it takes to implement that vision. In other words, the skill set that is real does not match up with what is proposed in the dream state. Being honest with yourself is a strength, not a weakness. Being overconfident about the process of starting a business often eliminates outside sources of information. Network resources are definitely diminished because of this behavior. Being humble about your discovery is a strength that lasts throughout the life of the business. Embrace it!

ENTITLEMENT AS A RATIONALE

Entitlements can emerge in the process when individuals use their past experiences as justification for starting a business. Some examples of Entitlements have to do with age, years of experience, and sacrifice, to name a few. How people feel about these thoughts is often shaped by perceived realities that are easy to justify, given that few challenges are faced in the dream state. The reasons for this are two-fold. Either they are not openly expressed, or no one in the storyline is there to ask critical questions or tell you that you're wrong. The result is a free-flowing fantasy that has no boundaries. It then festers into a reality that is often unrealistic and unattainable. So, if a person feels entitled to start a business due to their age or years of experience, it can lead to disaster without intervention by an information process or an informed person. The rationale of entitlement is also an outgrowth of the rationale of overconfidence. Because of the presence of the rationale of entitlement, shortcuts are often justified. Inputs to the information process are frequently overlooked due to the perception that they are unnecessary.

Another example of this entitlement idea has to do with family businesses. If a family has a business and a child is influenced by its success, it could lead to feelings of entitlement. Ideas like readiness, maturity, or educational preparedness may be pushed aside prematurely. There is a reason why succession is complicated. It takes a great deal of effort to have family members take over or start new businesses. Assuming your children will have all the necessary ingredients to continue or start a new business is a stretch. Evidence of this idea is prevalent throughout all industries. Generally, only 30% of family businesses survive into the second generation. And with third-generation family businesses, only 12% survive. Much of this inability to pass on the family business has to do with the heirs.

In some cases, no heirs were born to take over the business. When there are heirs, few qualify to operate the business. Given these odds, it is clear that even the best-educated heirs could not manage the family business. It takes planning and the experience of operating the company to have any chance of success. The same applies to those who feel entitled because they belong to a family business. There is no substitute for knowledge, skills, and abilities when it comes to entrepreneurship. And let's not forget about mentality and the tenacity to want to start a business. Having continuity is a treasured commodity in entrepreneurship. One thing it is not would be the idea that it is an entitlement. Put that idea on the shelf and forget about it.

As you will see, there are many obstacles to the successful launch of a business. One of the most disturbing obstacles has to do with what I refer to as potholes in the vision.

POTHOLES IN THE VISION

People love to see the results of an entrepreneur's work, but are often shocked when they discover the level of risk taken to achieve those results. It is often necessary to leverage capital to make the purchases necessary to achieve that dream. Where will the startup money come from? How will you communicate your vision to the business community? If you develop a product, how will you warranty it? It's these little potholes in your business platform that tend to cripple the launch, given the lack of coverage in the dream state. There is also the lack of inclusion in the business plan, which is what creates that frustration. Since it is a preventable mistake, the result of leaving out parts of the analysis can be fatal to the progress of the startup.

For example, I shared with you an example of the manufacturer in Part I. I mentioned that there was a machine there. So, using the machine-in-the-garage vision, how does that machine get purchased? Where will the money come from to buy raw materials? How about utilities like electricity and water? These are but a few items that are considered potholes. It is these so-called pot holes in the decision process that need to be filled with the conduit material found in the discovery period. And let's be clear, those items are identified only through an estimate found in other businesses. In other words, it's an amount that is benchmarked, not an actual number. What if the forecast is inaccurate? That is why I refer to it as a pothole. It's hard to see, but when it comes, it creates a bump in the ride. Some ideas can create obstacles to launching your business. The following ideas relate to the perception of what it is like to be an entrepreneur. Having unrealistic expectations can be detrimental to the journey of launching your business. Those unrealistic expectations can be produced through the fantasies of riches and fame.

THE FANTASY OF RICHES AND FAME

The internet of ideas has provided exactly that—ideas. Whether those ideas are factual, realistic, or successful is often not known to the reader. Most are looking to pique your interest so that they can sell you the latest idea of how to become a successful entrepreneur. Many talk about being successful, but few ever offer legitimate training that leads to successful launches. Books and website access are sold to expose you to all these wonderful seminars and reading material. Who would not be in support of such a service? But ask yourself, what are they really selling? Do your homework on what you need to know and direct your research toward that which advances your vision. Filling you up with get-rich-quick stories and hot opportunities rarely helps in your business launch.

Other aspects of sensationalistic thinking that are viewed as startup opportunities are the study of wealthy entrepreneurs who sell their books and websites to inspire people to start businesses. This segment of the startup process is also influenced by the reality of who is typically regarded as a successful entrepreneur. Consider that some individuals may have family backgrounds that have contributed to their current level of success. I can confidently say that the degree of protocol required to access the information necessary for a career as a performer or entrepreneur has different pathways. Modeling yourself after a wealthy entrepreneur who sells books and tapes on success rarely leads to a successful launch. Learning how to produce your own resources of information is better understood and usually leads to a longer-lasting flow of information. Longevity in information flow helps to identify when to shift resources, change a service mix, or further brand yourself with a new product or service. It's a powerful tool that you need to build. While using individuals who sell books and web access as role models can be fun, you lack the resource platform to operate on the same level as they do when launching a business. So, let's get our heads in the game. Let's get started with the work and stop looking for shortcuts or elevated superficial profiles that have little chance of succeeding. Given your current financial circumstances and your network of influencers, a more realistic approach to your launch is based on what you create. It is not from what is created for you.

There is another example of this fantasy that is delivered to you during the time in the dream state. Those ideas can be transformed into reality if you allow them to happen through your conscious self. Certainly, sensationalism has an open door in the dream state. Specific common ideas that emerge from this vision in the dream state can interfere with your launch. Here are some common ideas:

- Do you see yourself surrounded by things like houses, cars, and such?
- Are you sitting in a plush office as president of a company?
- Do you live in a mansion?
- Are you dreaming of being rich or famous through your business?

Many dreams are like this, where there is little substance other than the feeling of being wealthy and free of a work schedule. From these visions come these fallacies that can become deeply rooted in your subconscious. And they then can show up in our everyday thinking

Here are some examples of fallacies that exist in the Dream State that often transfer to reality:

- Entrepreneurs are all wealthy.
- Entrepreneurs live on golf courses and play golf often.
- Entrepreneurs work when they want
- Entrepreneurs take numerous vacations throughout the year

In my experience, entrepreneurs work long hours, and many have initial incomes that are less than what they made when they left Corporate America. Many do not golf or live on golf courses. And vacation time is something that comes with years of successful management. It takes time to train a staff of people to run your company while you are gone.

It's this inability to separate fiction from reality in the dream state that paralyzes the dreamer from operationalizing the vision. When reality is discovered, it becomes a fork-in-the-road moment. Be careful not to be mesmerized by this type of vision. Be careful not to be vulnerable to programs where you pay money to relive that utopia of riches and benefit models. Many of these schemas unravel themselves in a conference room at some hotel, where the message is sweet, including the chocolate chip cookies. Incorporate only that which supports your pathway to transition. Forget about the fantasies. They are obstacles to your development as an entrepreneur.

Another item on the list of obstacles is the dependence on social media and the website maintenance trap.

THE SOCIAL MEDIA AND WEBSITE TRAP

The social media and website trap takes place because of where we are as a society. We communicate through digitized means to accomplish our goals. Although I am not opposed to the use of these instruments, I believe entrepreneurs looking to rationalize their business idea may find it beneficial to share it with their social media network. Or, maybe creating a website could be a way to gauge whether you would attract any traffic by sharing a glimpse of your business online. My response is NO! There is so much more that needs to be learned before pushing out ideas about your business. This idea has not been tested and may not pan out after further exploration of the marketplace. Remember, once you place something out in the digitized world, it remains long after its usefulness. Instead, have a branding platform established before walking out with your story. It is rare for feasibility to be accomplished through social media or websites.

The other part of the trap is the ongoing maintenance required to manage your website and social media sites. Once you decide to utilize social media sites and a website for your business, a time commitment is required. Starting social media sites or a website to communicate with your markets requires you to manage those sites. Many entrepreneurs start communicating this way but fail to follow through over time. Many of those instruments become personal play toys or abandoned communication devices that actually begin to work against the company. An example of this abandonment would be the failure to answer queries that are made on your webpage. Not answering inquiries in a timely fashion. Not updating the website with new developments in the company. Many entrepreneurs decided to utilize these communication devices without a plan to manage them. These are part of your marketing effort. They should not be utilized until a plan is formulated for their use. The obstacle arises when you have to start explaining to prospects and influencers why your website is dormant. It also applies to the question of why your social media site is inactive. Now, where are you spending your time?

After considering the behavioral issues and the propensity-for-risk principle, along with all the work necessary to address feasibility, you may be ready to take the plunge into starting your own business. After considering all of the obstacles that could interfere with your launch, you may be prepared for the next step. This next transition I refer to as stepping into the abyss. Given the characteristics of the experience you are about to receive, this step takes courage in believing in yourself. It is here that a commitment is made time-wise and certainly expense-wise when you step into the Abyss! Are you ready?

Takeaways from Part II:

- A diverse set of people start businesses. Some people work harder than others due to differences in personality type.
- Corporate environmental attributes are not necessarily strengths in transitioning to the world of entrepreneurship
- Starting a business requires individuals to address all functions of the business. Rarely does an individual have proficiency in all the functions.
- Educational programs are essential in addressing all the knowledge needed to implement a business plan effectively
- The propensity-for-risk principle is a barometer that measures the ability to handle risk. It is also a determinant in the successful life of the entrepreneur.
- Establishing the feasibility of your business completes the process of establishing your vision
- There are many rationales used to substitute for establishing feasibility. No rationale effectively addresses the establishment of the feasibility of a business idea

- Little details in the process of starting a business can end up determining the success of the business
- Fantasies exist in every world, including entrepreneurship. They remain in the same composition within every world. They are fantasies, not principles.
- Social media and website usage should be implemented with caution, given the workload it brings to your daily activities

III

STEPPING INTO THE ABYSS

Stepping into the abyss requires some level of preparation on the part of the entrepreneur. I would label this requirement as a toolbox approach to this next step. Examples of what a toolbox is includes preparing a business plan. Everything that you learned in completing a picture of the details surrounding your vision can be recorded in a business plan. What is addressed in a business plan has to do with the following items:

- Executive summary
- Products and services
- The marketing plan
- The organization and management plan
- The operating plan
- The financial plan
- A SWOT analysis (Strengths, Weaknesses, Opportunities, and Threats)
- Break-even analysis
- Start-up summary

There are many versions of what is addressed in a business plan. These items listed are generic in that all must be addressed to cover the necessary functions within a start-up operation. You could take a course in entrepreneurship, attend a seminar on building a business plan, or start working in the industry to gain more knowledge and experience. What is not part of the toolbox approach is to simply start the business with the idea that the learning will take place along the way. Individuals who decide to wing it usually do so because of their impatience to start the business. Others wing it because they are experiencing anxiety from doing nothing about their dreams for years. Remember from Part II when the idea that the entrepreneur's age starts to become an issue, and the feeling of urgency begins to replace the conditions of feasibility. Other reasons I have discovered are centered on procrastination due to the inability to get the business started. And lastly, let's face it. It takes a lot of work to complete a business plan. So with your toolbox in hand and your motivation to step forward, it's time to introduce you to the abyss.

THE TERMS OF THE ABYSS

Stepping into the abyss is a life event that challenges everything you have ever thought about regarding your business idea. From that crossover moment, an evaluation process begins that is now real. When visualizing your business idea, you had the opportunity to reset the circumstances and address any adverse outcomes or unsatisfactory results. That reversal of events in the storyline is no longer possible in the abyss. There are now real consequences to your decision-making that can only be reversed through further investment or realized losses. For instance, if you misread the market and experience a drought for your product or service, the consequences are clear: reduced revenue. If you had planned to achieve a particular level of sales over time, a pivot would be necessary to compensate for the reduced revenue. That would mean a loan from the bank at some point, or creating another source of revenue to fill in the gap expected from your efforts. Now, multiply those situations by all the potential issues in your planning, and you could be in deep trouble quickly. You cannot blink and erase all that faces you. There is no reset in the real world. With that said, let's walk into the abyss.

As you walk through that door into the abyss, you will experience a room full of floating opportunities, changing variables, and behavioral moments that will be a bit different than what was experienced during the dream state. Your experience could be anything from a shocking experience to a calming one. I consider that a scale with everything else in between. In other words, everything is possible, and you will need to deal with all of it throughout that initial period of consciousness in the abyss. Being ready for this step into the abyss does not come about in an organized, easy-to-interpret format. It is a random set of moments that cultivates a presence in your mind. So, how does all of that come about? The first place to start is to go back to your conscious state of mind.

THE CONSCIENCE MINDSET

When deciding to launch your business idea, your confidence in yourself is overwhelming. You believe in yourself. You can research no more as to whether what you want to do is feasible because you are convinced that it is. Your adrenaline is running strong. Your nightly dreams reinforce your decision to launch your business. You are ready to move on from your current work life and experience what it is like to be self-employed.

These feelings are normal. Who would not be excited about launching a business? Not only are you confident in yourself, but that confidence is creating a motivation to step forward and begin the process of separating yourself from your old life. From working for someone else, where you are an employee, to being the owner of a business, the excitement could not be more exhilarating. And all of that sweat equity that has been applied to creating this business idea motivates you to go forward. And, given that there is no absolute signal that what you know is an ironclad recipe for success, your decision to step forward can be justified by that rationale. Why not now? But caution is in the wind. Being overwhelmed with joy and happiness is wonderful until it becomes a pothole, as it was explained in Part II. The need for quick gratification often leads to poor decision-making. With poor decision-making comes mistakes. With mistakes come disappointments. I suggest that you be cautious about getting too far ahead of yourself. Instead, take the process in steps to ensure that your readiness has a solid platform to build from and execute a launch that is planned, not rushed. This conscious mindset is important to understand since it will be your filter for everything that comes from the abyss. You will judge what comes your way through your current mindset. But what should you do next? How do you proceed with the launch? Let's define what the abyss is first and then explain how it can affect your conscious self and your overall business launch.

A Definition of the Abyss

Stepping into the abyss is an experience that is never forgotten, nor is it anything one can escape from; it's permanent. What does that mean exactly?

If one searches for why the word "abyss" is used here, there are evil definitions of the word, and there are others. My use of the word has to do with this definition:

Abyss refers to a deep void or chasm, either literal or figurative.

You can find this definition in dictionaries and on websites. But what does it have to do with entrepreneurship? Is entrepreneurship that negative of an experience? Is entrepreneurship a bottomless pit of hell? One might have to ask the definition of hell first before applying it to entrepreneurship. I am not suggesting that being in business for yourself is like a bottomless pit in hell. Without preparation, launching a business can create a mixture of hellish moments that are not comfortable due to the uncertainties that exist.

Defining the abyss requires an understanding of the changing environment that exists within the abyss. This discussion should give you some idea of how to think about the abyss. Many have stepped into the abyss and experienced a quicksand-like behavior, simply because too much happens at the same time. Other reactions may be described through the following descriptions: Lack of preparation, unrealistic expectations, fatigue, emotional distress, and bewilderment. But why? What actually happens to cause it to be an abyss? Why are there so many types of reactions to this environment?

First, realize that no book, no study, no guru can absolutely prepare you for what you will experience in starting your business because no one can predict the future. No one can control all the variables that exist at one time in a space called life. And variables that are known change over time in unpredictable ways. For example, there are those individuals who will share their experience in starting a business with you, and we should thank them for their time. But let's break down the reality they are sharing by using my experience as an example. I was in the Financial Securities business for thirty-four years. When I started my business, the political and regulatory environments were very different than what exists today. The business platform for getting started also changed during that period. Years ago, if you wanted to be a financial advisor, you could begin in a part-time format and grow from there. That model is dead today. The amount of paperwork needed to open accounts has grown exponentially. This means that small accounts are no longer profitable for the beginning advisor. This variable makes the start-up process much more difficult. Sharing my journey from starting my business to progressing through the ranks may not be particularly useful for someone looking to launch a financial services business today. So, variables like expectations of income or workload and work time are very different ingredients today than what I encountered getting started. So, things change over time, and the predictability of how it will directly or indirectly affect your business is a lesson in humility because even the gurus get it wrong. Another interpretation of the abyss can be formulated through the concept of chaos theory.

THE PRESENCE OF CHAOS THEORY

You should not be discouraged by how the abyss operates. It is merely a phenomenon that lacks a clear operational plan. Understand that the inputs that you take in through your network do not always add up to absolute positive or useful criteria for success. This is why the term 'void' is so pertinent in the definition of the abyss. The interaction of variables that seem to be similar can lead to different outcomes over time. This is a challenge that takes place throughout your entire life as an entrepreneur.

I can apply the concept of chaos theory to explain the term abyss further. The definition is as follows:

From the internet or an AI query, chaos theory explores how seemingly random or unpredictable behavior can

arise from a simple deterministic system, emphasizing that even small changes in initial conditions can lead to drastically different outcomes over time.

Chaos theory, then, can be utilized to describe the environment that you will encounter regardless of what markets you are working with. For example, the marketing strategies that you employ today that were discovered as successful in your research may not have the same level of success in your current marketplace. Said in another way, just because something has worked in the past and generated income has little bearing or influence on what will generate that same level of business or revenue in the future. This is not to scare you off, but consider this idea. Nothing is forever, and nothing applied is guaranteed to work forever. And why? Applied to the business environment, things and behavior change over time. Our reactions to product offerings change by age. Societal needs change through the generations. The use of the product may change in a direction that could not have been predicted given the information available at the time of its creation. A perfect example is how the apparel market works. Changing fashions from year to year and by age would challenge any planner to always have it right. The right designs, colors, and advertising, combined with the right amount of material and labor to meet all planning initiatives, are truly impressive.

This is why chaos theory applies to our business environment. It's the random behavior that can emerge that challenges business owners to pivot to a new reality. It forces entrepreneurs to shift resources to accommodate the change. It can also cause entrepreneurs to redistribute resources to meet demand and invest capital in areas forecasted to complement their business model. One example that is apparent here is how the auto industry was taken by storm by two styles of automobiles. Consumers decided at some point in the business cycle to purchase SUVs and trucks. The requirement to manufacture these models and limit the production of other lines of product is called a pivot to the new reality. It also incorporates the action of shifting resources to accommodate the change in consumer preferences. Think of the redistribution of resources to meet the demand of the consumer. Capital was needed to make the shift to meet this new demand from the consumer.

So with all that said, what does it actually mean for a person just getting a business started? How is this useful to a person who couldn't give a damn about theories and abstract thoughts about the process? Perhaps some examples will help to visualize what this means to a person starting a business. Let's dig deeper into the world of chaos theory.

THE TOOLBOX IN DEALING WITH CHAOS THEORY

The most efficient way to deal with chaos theory or the abyss in general is through a concerted effort to be a student of the market. That effort requires the entrepreneur to be actively involved in gathering information. This brings us back to the concept of grasping the conduit idea. Few can survive the initial stages of a business launch without a centralized system or platform to gather and process information. It's part of the toolbox approach. Questions like:

- How will you know who your competitors are?
- How do you gather information that is pertinent to your business?
- Where will that conduit of information come from?

I can assure you, it will not come up and slap you in the face. It does not create itself. It will not speak to you in your dreams. The only controller behind this operation is you! The data gathering process is the responsibility of the entrepreneur, whether they gather it themselves or pay someone to collect it for them. There are service providers that will deliver valuable information to business owners in their industry. The most valuable information for businesspeople launching a business is the effort and knowledge they invest. At the outset of your business, you are a small microorganism of activity in a market that may have many players or organizations offering similar services. And, if your idea is something no one provides, that too speaks loudly as to its position and importance in the market. Said another way, whether your idea is already offered in the market or not, both conditions provide information that is useful during your launch. It all begins with your reading of the marketplace. Trying to figure out what consumers want is a hill many business owners climb daily. Here is an example. Online apps are looked at from both sides of this problem. Some consumers do not see the need for a phone app, but many purchase them with the intent to utilize them one day.

Given that the scenario is based on a want and a need, how do entrepreneurs consider developing phone apps that involve such complex dynamics? Some will tell you that it becomes a numbers game and a firm just needs to keep creating apps with the idea that some will be successful and others will die on the shelf. So that demand situation drives the market, and those who want to participate by starting a business have to accept those terms or move on to something else. You might ask why. The answer lies in the understanding of the alternative to that market strategy. If an entrepreneur decides to produce only a limited number of apps, expecting all to be hits, the results may lead to disappointing revenue numbers. This market strategy would be considered highly risky. So the entrepreneur has a choice. That choice profile can either allow such activity to accept higher risks or motivate them to adapt to the circumstance by incorporating it in the business plan. It is not your place to be an activist early in your role as an entrepreneur. Understanding how your markets work is a foundation for ideas that create change. That requires the entrepreneur to be a student of the market.

There are numerous examples of how consumers incorporate product and service offerings into their everyday lives. With that said, every movement and new piece of data that affects the production and implementation of what you are in business to provide can be and will be affected at some point in time by the change in such information. The conduit-of-information system then allows you the opportunity to extract that information from the market through an organized platform of interventions. These interventions yield the results needed to activate strategies that pivot, reorganize, shift, and re-create the apparatus you need to survive. The platform of interventions is closely tied to your network of influencers. It also includes your research protocol, which is enacted to identify the components of your planned intervention.

Planning interventions is an action that operates independently. In other words, without effort, there can be little expected results. One motivating force that will affect everything that you do is built on the rules behind the abyss.

Rules of the Abyss

The idea of walking into the abyss and experiencing the changing variables and behaviors that I spoke about earlier should now have more relevance to its effect on you. Once you walk into the abyss, the door closes, and your world begins to change. Whether you like the environment or not has nothing to do with your purpose now. Your purpose now is to launch your business. If you decide to walk back through the door into the dream state, there are behavioral consequences to such a decision. An individual may feel that the launch was a waste of time or that they were not ready for it. This recoiling behavior has consequences. What if you quit your job to make the launch? What if you borrowed money or used your own money to make the launch? What happens if other people are involved with you? What are they supposed to do now? Once you enter the abyss, you find yourself in a permanent state of reality where every decision has a resulting consequence or action that can have positive and negative results. This is why it's considered a motivating force that affects everything.

If you decide to walk back through the door of the abyss, the abyss will follow you. How would that happen? It happens because you now have to rationalize why you failed to make a successful launch. Now you have to explain to others why it did not work out. Now you have to find a rationale to survive the fallout that can be felt behaviorally. And now you have to maintain the business requirements for tax and regulatory purposes. And now, instead of experiencing the haunting of our perceived reality, you will experience the haunting of your actual reality. I think you get the message here. Avoid this situation. Once through the door, proceed with the motivation you came with.

Now that was a lot of information to swallow. But it was necessary to give you the idea of how important the launch is to you psychologically. It should also identify what the abyss is and how to survive it. But what can you do to understand the effects of the abyss? Is there a tool that can help provide some direction?

THE SIGNALING TOOL

In explaining why chaos theory is a good description of the abyss, let's return to the data-gathering system that I spoke about earlier. Well, that same system can act as a signaling tool within the abyss. Let's ask a few questions about that system.

- First, what is the source of your information?
- How does this source of information help you monitor the business taking place in your market?
- Is it reliable over time?
- Is it difficult to retrieve?
- Does it help you differentiate your business from others in the industry?
- What are you doing today to place yourself in a position to extract that data? In the initial stages of your launch, this activity should help you develop competitive products and services that match your competitors. But what if you have not secured such a place? How can you build a system that will help monitor and make informed decisions in this market?
- What date gathering system will help build a strategy to confront the challenges faced within the abyss? Remember the chaos theory example I gave and how important it is to understand the possible reasons for the continuing fluctuations in market behavior?

Extracting information from a market takes time and effort. Patience is also necessary to avoid anxiety and inaccurate interpretations of the information you have collected. There is no button to push. This is where networking becomes a valuable tool, playing a crucial role in staying current in your market. It is also a signaling tool that helps differentiate your business from others and provides a current method of discovery. Let's examine this process.

Finding relevant business networks can be challenging, especially when you assume you have no prior experience with them as an entrepreneur. You may have come to know about them through your corporate role, but that is considerably different than where you are headed. Corporate people often attend events in these networks as a task obligation from their companies to check the box for community involvement. Your role is much different. You are there to observe, track competitor offerings, connect with possible customers, and build a brand around yourself as a responsible and active business owner. This strengthens the argument that corporate life does not adequately prepare you for entrepreneurship. By compiling information about your local competitors, you can begin to build a profile of the product and service models available to customers. And, you guessed it, from there you can differentiate, shape, and build your own product or service model that is informed and constructed with real data, not dreams!

The other aspect of having your hand on the conduit of information is through research. Few owners have actually told me how they enjoy digging into the research for ideas. What I am referring to is not a full-blown research project but one that monitors secondary data sources. These sources cover issues related to your industry. Whether it's restaurants, engineering firms, law firms, accounting firms, janitorial service firms, or you name it, there is a journal of information that is generated to appeal to you. You are their customer. It's time to get busy in those channels to extract information to get moving toward a position in the industry you have chosen.

So, after stepping into the research process, what's next? Understand that when I used the word "patience," I did not do so lightly. Perhaps I should have used the bold print or capitalized it. All too often, entrepreneurs get antsy. They want things to happen quickly. Pushing the market is not advisable. One should pull the market, meaning that you are doing enough to be recognized as a player. Sitting back and waiting for something to happen is the corporate version of the process. Thinking like an entrepreneur, you get up and seize opportunities to help people recognize what you are offering. You also make the collection of data an everyday activity that transforms you into an expert in your market. An example would be as follows:

- Your understanding of how your market works
- The major players
- Products and services commonly offered

Where do you stand in terms of the ingredients that contribute to better decision-making? In other words, be proactive in extracting information. You will be in a role that requires proactive decision-making. You will now make things happen. This perspective illustrates the difference between a corporate perspective and an entrepreneurial perspective.

After moving forward with the extraction of information process, one might get to a point where there is a feeling of accomplishment. You may start to feel as if you are a major player in your industry. You may also begin to think of your work as a batting average, as in baseball. In other words, you have some winners and some losers. This can be a bittersweet turning point for you. Understanding this situation requires a visit back to chaos theory. I delve into this phenomenon through an explanation of the scorecard.

THE SCORECARD

As we progress in gathering information and developing marketing strategies, we eventually reach a point where we experience defeat or unexpected results from the launch. Let's hope everything went well, but often, it's not perfect, and the reasons for the lag in success have to do with what? I mentioned chaos theory first for a reason. You may have copied an activity from another competitor that has been successful for them. Radio programs are a fine example of this idea. Entrepreneurs may think that being on the radio will generate huge sales because of market penetration. To think that this would be a quick way to become known is where the fallacy comes in. Remember the idea about patience? Be ready to exhibit it. And be prepared to pay for it. Financial resources are usually limited at the start of the business. So why do entrepreneurs make this mistake of using tools they cannot afford early in the launch of their business? Impatience comes to mind.

Chamber of commerce memberships are another example that comes to mind. Expecting quick results from these networking activities is a failed strategy that leads to disappointment. The cost of participating alone can be troublesome if networking strategies are not positioned as a long-term strategy for visibility and branding purposes.

Be careful not to over-read the scorecard. The same would hold true of the success you are having early in the launch. You want to enjoy it. But reacting to a small time frame of success is like looking at the football field from the five-yard line. The scorecard is a moving target that tends to fluctuate over time. There is a reason why companies rely on quarterly results, annual reports, and three- and five-year forecasts.

After some time in the business, I believe you will gain a deeper understanding of chaos theory and why the word "abyss" is used to describe your marketplace. In addition to chaos theory, though, other factors determine results. Those factors have a lot to do with you.

FACTORS TO CONSIDER

Let's now take a different direction on the idea of the launch. This direction touches on uncertainty, risk, the entrepreneur's temperament, the role of the entrepreneur, and what makes corporate life different from being a business owner.

Failure is part of the process for success. No matter how much information you collect, there will always be the possibility that it may not have been as helpful as you initially thought. You took every measure to make sure your information was accurate. Your decisions were measured, and your efforts were massive off the charts. However, in cases of uncertainty, the correlation between using that information and achieving high sales numbers is often not strong enough to yield the desired result. And, it's hard to know exactly what to expect because predicting the future has challenges. Perfection does not exist. There is a reason why corporate models of planning utilize a high-outcome-low outcome-probable-outcome planning apparatus. This is a gauge system that predicts results based on a parameter of possible outcomes from the implementation of a business or market strategy. It recognizes exactly what I have shared with you, that every action within the abyss can have different outcomes over time. Planning for those outcomes is prudent given the coverage of possibilities addressed and the knowledge expressed from such measures. This model of planning expresses a level of expertise needed to complete the scenario, which requires research. The entrepreneur can apply the same research process to make projections and plan accordingly.

What separates entrepreneurs from employees can often be expressed in three words: Assumes personal risk. There are other ways to express this same behavior. For example, the entrepreneur assumes risk by challenging uncertainty. When trials of intervention fail, the entrepreneur learns from such situations and applies that learning to the next scenario. Corporate people do the same thing. The problem with that opinion is that entrepreneurs are risking their own capital during that moment of learning; employees get paid through corporate assets to learn. And the sting from a monetary mistake may result in the entrepreneur not being paid that week or month because there are no assets left to disburse. Not the same for corporate professionals.

And then there's the successful launch, where everything goes well, and you are on your way to building the business. The temperament here is to keep your head. Spend only what you have to and begin to accumulate funds for further business opportunities. Many entrepreneurs want to celebrate their early success. Keep in mind, as I learned in baseball, you're ahead in the first inning with 8 to go.

So, during your launch, you can experience success, while others may be less successful. Regardless of the initial outcome, there will be moments of correction where your business model will be tweaked and adjusted to reflect the discoveries. That will be a process that is eternal in the world of entrepreneurship. No action lasts forever. The changing markets, changing behaviors of consumers, and much more can warrant a change in business model, as was discussed earlier.

Another aspect of the uncertainty/risk factor is the monetary effect on you. Spending money that does not yield the expected results can be painful. Welcome to entrepreneurship. Success, then, is to be appreciated and honored because it brings with it the other side of reality. How will you hold up under those circumstances that would be considered failures or miscalculations? It's what drains the energy from many aspiring entrepreneurs. They have difficulty with failure. If this is the case, your life as an entrepreneur will be limited. Even after the initial launch, there will be moments of disappointment. The temperament of the entrepreneur is the key to utilizing those moments as learning scenarios. No matter how many years of success you can experience, there will come a time when the data that you collected and applied did not yield the results you were looking for. It happens. Chaos theory is alive and well. How you internalize and execute the results of the intervention in the market is critical to your survival. This is where the cliché comes in; one needs to develop a thick skin.

So, as you navigate the start-up landscape, be aware that some disconnects and aberrations make the process challenging. You, as a business owner, will face the abyss as long as you are in business. Rather than running or cowering to defend yourself, it's time to switch the perspective. It's time to go on the offensive, as it's been said in business circles. When you make the switch and challenge the aberration with a counter strategy or a shift in direction, you begin to live the life of an entrepreneur. You begin to understand that your start-up is only the beginning of a metamorphosis that is building inside of you and within the business you started.

In the next section, we will continue the adventure of living in the abyss and becoming a formidable force in the world of entrepreneurship. Branding is a process that is essential to your continued success as an entrepreneur. Understanding the implications of the branding process can determine how successful you will be as an entrepreneur.

Takeaways from Part III:

- The marketplace (abyss) is more of a phenomenon than a concrete element
- The mindset of the entrepreneur is key to addressing the challenges of the marketplace
- Chaos theory is a good descriptor of how the marketplace operates
- Research protocols are one of the most effective tools used to address marketplace challenges
- Knowing and understanding the rules of the marketplace will reduce the possibility of having a negative start-up
- Networking is a signaling tool used to evaluate current marketing and operational plans

- Over-celebrating early success can lead to poor decision-making. Be realistic about your early success
- Temperament and interpretative skills go a long way in keeping the reality of your business intact

IV

A BEHAVIORAL FOOTPRINT IN ESTABLISHING AND MAINTAINING YOUR BRAND

In Part III, you were introduced to the idea of the marketplace as the abyss. The abyss was defined by utilizing chaos theory as a way to identify the complicated environment entrepreneurs face in the initial launch of a business. In Part IV, the subject shifts to incorporate behaviors that occur after the entrepreneur achieves a measure of success. To accomplish that objective, a discussion of how brands are formulated would help you understand the journey you are experiencing.

Now that the launch is complete, you are living the dream. Right? Let's hope that you feel that way. You have invested a lot of time into this venture, and it's time to have some rewards for all of that sweat. Having fun is okay, but be aware that the work you do now is crucial for supporting all that you have already built in the launch. Establishing and maintaining your image is not easy. And let's face it, early on in the life of an entrepreneur, your image is all that you have to offer. Not enough time has passed for your product or service to gain traction and remove you from the front line. And even after your products or services are recognized, your image will still be critical to the reputation of the business. So, your image and rhetoric are being evaluated by the business community. Whether you realize it or not, you are under the microscope. This is why it is important to set a plan to establish yourself in the business community and the marketplace.

ESTABLISHING YOURSELF

During the time of your launch, you planned to stick to the business plan, implement what you have dreamt about, and realize its virtues. And although expectations are probably running high, you don't know what the outcome will be, given your knowledge of chaos theory. You do have expectations, though, and that is okay, given all the work that has been put into this venture.

To establish yourself as a business, your activity must align with the marketing materials developed from the business plan. Next, the entrepreneur has to take a proactive approach to building an image in the community. Thus, the marketing materials are utilized as tools to help accomplish this goal. Some examples of building your image can be described through some of the work I cited earlier in the book. I referred to networking activities such as a chamber of commerce membership, social media interactions, and website maintenance activities. Let's not forget that the primary focus of your image building should be on your target market. Many entrepreneurs become overwhelmed by networks that lack potential clients or avenues for business growth. They are wasting time, energy, and money. And you may be having fun with these other networks. But when it comes time to pay the bills, this reality will be apparent. I recall a financial service representative who believed that showcasing a frugal lifestyle would persuade people to select him as their financial advisor. He involved himself with people who were curious about investing. He would spend a great deal of time educating them on everything he knew about finance. The problem is, he involved himself with people who had no real funds to invest. So, he had little revenue to show for his hours in the field talking to his network. And although he was a smart guy, he closed up the business after a year or so because he had to find a way to pay the bills! In financial services, your network must be a potential source of revenue. It seems simple, yet many individuals continue to fail at learning this lesson.

There was some coverage of this networking idea in the risk questionnaire I shared with you. Some questions explored the actions you need to take to initiate the networking process. For example, what will your workweek look like? Who are you going to see this week? Remember? That question process becomes an everyday mantra that is repeated using the elevator speech and marketing materials within the business plan.

Once your brand is formulated, apply a schematic of how to communicate it everywhere, including your website. Social media and website activities should be leveraged as opportunities to enhance the business's image further. And once prospects and clients start to visit your website, the chance to build your image expands tremendously. Your customers are your best marketing advocates, along with your network advocates. What are you doing today to communicate with them? And how are you communicating with them? Often, the central method of communicating is through a digitized communication piece.

THE DIGITIZED COMMUNICATION PIECE

This digitized communication piece works directly from the marketing plan set in the business plan. Social media has become a tool for reaching markets through a digitized instrument. A website, Facebook, Instagram, LinkedIn, or any other platform that suits your communication style is often part of a marketing strategy. But how will you draw traffic to those sites? What activities are you involved in daily to feed those instruments with ingredients that prospects need to learn from that expose them to your product or service offerings? Sharing your idea of starting a business on social media is not a good idea. Many aspects of your business could change. Formulating your brand through interactions within the abyss is far more productive than guessing what it might look like based on the initial business plan. This is why these learning episodes that take place early in the launch serve as adjustments to the original business plan. It also keeps the business plan relevant. I have often referred to this situation as the living business plan. Since it evolves and adapts to market discoveries, it keeps the ideas learned relevant to the overall business plan. Afterwards, the entrepreneur has a better chance of formulating the brand, given the fresh information gained from networking activities. From here, it's time to communicate its structure and market it to your target market. This is the beginning of formulating your brand.

FORMULATING YOUR BRAND

As time moves forward, your work with the community becomes visible. To understand how you can become a brand, let's explore all the various ideas that define what a brand is and how brands operate. I will also provide examples of companies that demonstrate how brands contribute to continued success. Let's start with some basic ideas about branding.

It was stated in Part III of this book that we live within the world of the abyss. It operates on its own wick and is seldom controllable for long. Whatever is placed in the marketplace concerning your image travels to numerous corners of the market. And especially, once you put a footprint in the social media marketplace, it becomes difficult to change or remove. Some evaluations of your image are placed there by you. Other evaluations are placed there by clients and your network advocates. Regardless, that image of you becomes your brand. As your business grows, the brand becomes more centered on the product than on you. It does not eliminate the need to support your image as its founder. Early in your launch, your image became your brand. When you stepped into the abyss, you became a brand. Whether it was intentional or not, it happened. There were conversations with people that centered on your background, experience, and capabilities. The image portrayed during that time was disseminated to the business community through your networking activities. A portrait was developed in the minds of other business professionals, as well as your social media footprint and website structure.

Just think for a moment about what people see when they interact with you. I refer to these items as symbols. It has to do with the clothes you wear, the car you drive, and where your office is located. It also has to do with the ease of use of your website and your availability online through social media. Let's not forget that some of you will have a storefront business that people witness when they come to purchase products and services from you. They will be looking around and evaluating how thorough the design of the facility is. Is it professional? Is it efficient? Is it user-friendly? That first impression matters. It's a reflection of you. The business community evaluates people based on the items that are currently in view. What do they see first in you? To continue my story about the financial service representative, he wanted to demonstrate to people how to be frugal. He wore simple clothes, was not color coordinated, drove an old car, and never invested in an advertising strategy. Wrong symbols, along with inadequate network contacts, led to the failure of the business. Few people want to do business with someone who does not look professional and successful.

This is especially true with the management of people's money. He did not address that concept.

So, after you are evaluated on the symbols that you have delivered to the community, the question of interest comes up. Are people interested in your business idea? If they are, questions about your product or service will be asked. This is a time to re-deliver your elevator speech about your company. If all goes well, people will be convinced to do business with you. They will become your customer. And if someone were to ask your customer to explain what you do, what would they say? The answer lies in what you conveyed to your customers during your interactions with them. It will also be reinforced through the content you share on social media and your website. They form a mental image of you and your business. It remains there until you change it. Customers then transfer that image to those they speak to and decide whether a referral is a possibility. All too often, entrepreneurs fail to update their websites to reflect the essence of their brand accurately. And if they decide to have a social media presence, they often fail to communicate frequently enough to be taken seriously. Like in golf, follow-through is important.

Through networking with other professionals, you can gain benefits by having them refer you to potential customers. These professionals are not your competitors. Like you, they are looking for customers through the networking process. This is why professional people network. In some circles, it's called business development because that is the purpose of their effort: to develop business opportunities.

To refresh your memory of information that was discussed in Part II, remember how networking was used during the feasibility process, where you are trying to identify competitors. Your goal was to gain insight into what your competitors offer regarding their product and service mix. From there, you compared your business idea to your competitors to get ideas about how your business will be different than what is currently available in the market. Through interactions with professionals who were not your competitors, they became advocates. Advocates refer potential customers to you. They have an idea about your brand, which is then sold to all potential customers who are referred. What is communicated to potential customers is determined by the content placed in the conduit-of-information portal (e.g., marketing material, website information, and social media interventions). That is your job to feed and maintain your image

Revisiting the customer referral and networking concept should re-emphasize the importance of establishing those contacts as you expand your business footprint. That footprint is known as your brand. Let's look further into the concept of branding to strengthen its role in your marketing effort..

BRANDING DEFINED FURTHER

Branding is a process that takes time to nurture and develop. It is not a toy to be played with whenever the next great idea comes along to change it. It exists in the minds of those who do business with you. Some companies have worked for years to develop their brands. They are consistent. The experience that the customer has with these companies is influential enough to earn repeat business. The customer's expectations are met every time they do business with that company. The mechanics of building that brand were delicate and needed to be managed carefully to be successful. Let's utilize some companies that exemplify the brand concept.

McDonald's

The establishment of McDonald's was not easy. It took years to build the brand as a fast food restaurant. People at that time (1953) had no idea what fast food was or what it was supposed to be. One thing is for certain: the golden arches became a symbol of its product line. The restaurant was open 24 hours a day. Consumers were puzzled about this. Who wants a hamburger in the morning? Many consumers did not think the restaurant chain would make it. Things changed over the years. The menu changed slowly. Through perseverance and consistency of purpose, McDonald's became the largest fast food chain in the world. And the symbol that we all know about is the golden arches. Even toddlers in the back seat of a car know what those arches mean now.

Some years ago, McDonald's tried to change its image to a healthy fast food restaurant. It failed to make the transition. It was returned to its roots by the public's purchasing power. Consumers continued to buy the items from the traditional menu rather than the healthy choices offered. The customer's view of McDonald's did not accept the new image. The public wanted fast food regardless of whether it was healthy or not. McDonald's decided to reverse course and made changes to the menu. Its brand still prevailed, and McDonald's continued to flourish even in the midst of aggressive marketing strategies from its competitors. It demonstrates the power of a company's image and how branding can affect consumer behavior.

Starbucks

We know the brand. Most of us who have been around a while would have come to the same conclusion about Starbucks. Who wants coffee all day long? And who would be interested in the various concoctions that Starbucks has come up with to entice the public to drink its coffee? But Starbucks established its brand and extended its coverage to restaurants and grocery stores without compromising its brand identity. People buy the coffee through many venues. Consumers make purchasing decisions based on brand recognition rather than where the product is purchased. Many companies have followed this same marketing strategy (e.g., Central Market, LaMadeleine's, and Dunkin' Donuts). Starbucks has now become more than a brand. For some, it has become a way of life.

Intuit

Intuit is another brand that continues to thrive in the industry. From a simple software provider to now a household name for tax and bookkeeping work, it has built its brand as a tool for industry professionals as well as everyday consumers. It has evolved into a leasing company that provides analytical support. It did so because the market for ongoing software support changed. Database companies like ACT implemented the same product strategy, which forced companies to follow that model change to survive. This model change placed tremendous financial pressure on consumers. Yet Intuit survived because of its ability to sell its brand over multiple markets. To explain further, before becoming a leasing company, Intuit was a software company where consumers purchased its product on a disc. Intuit then supported that product for many years without any further purchase by the consumer. I am referring to the QuickBooks product line. Then the change took place. Now, consumers lease the software that they purchase. They receive technical support as long as there is an active lease. When the purchase anniversary date comes, it's time to buy the product again for the next year of use and support. Although Intuit may have lost some customers due to the financial burden, the brand itself fostered a continuation of consumers purchasing the product and utilizing the service mix.

Apple

If ever there was an example of a brand that has become a way of life, it's the Apple line of products. This brand is generational. People followed the company through many iterations of phone technology. In addition, the introduction of the Mac computer and the IPad were innovations outside of phone technology, yet consumers continued to follow the company and embraced its brand. Consumers also recognized the AirPods headphones, Apple Watch, Apple TV and other technological products that continue to meet the demands of its customers. With all of the competition coming from other providers (i.e. Android phone line), Apple continues to benefit from its reputation and brand recognition.

I could go on and on about the many brands that you recognize as a consumer. Those brands did not get there by mistake. They were built through a strategy directed at prospective markets. The examples I have provided demonstrate the health of a secure brand. This influences the company's ability to withstand the many challenges of the business cycle. It can also survive through periods of dissatisfaction with product and service changes. Without a secure brand, the chance of losing customers can increase to the point of putting the business in a detrimental state.

Now that I have made my points about branding and the importance of establishing it, let's now examine a behavior that begins to show itself when considering a change in direction for the business. It's called brand expansion.

BRAND EXPANSION

When a business launch is early in its lifecycle, establishing the business is paramount to its ability to survive thereafter. If changes are made early in the brand platform, there could be the impression that the business is not yet stable enough to refer people to or to do business with. The impression can lead to the image that the business is not a viable vendor or business to embrace. The business owner then has to strengthen the brand to withstand any doubt. This is why making too many changes early in your development as a brand is dangerous and should be avoided. Managing the brand carefully will make sure your brand is solid in the minds of the business community and with your customer base. Another look at the subject of patience is in order.

PATIENCE

Patience is not an easy behavior to hold on to when you are itching to expand your business by making changes. Through the initial success of that business idea, knowledge may have been discovered that sparks interest in a different market, an extended product line, or a service mix. The question is, should you pursue other business opportunities so early in the development of your recently launched business? Or should you be patient and give your initial strategies a chance to work? Not an easy decision to make. It could be that your original analysis of the marketplace was wrong. You have now discovered that by actually interacting with it. Perhaps your marketing strategies aren't working, and you're considering alternative ways to reach customers. It also has to do with market cycles. Your launch could be enacted during a time when business is in a low cycle, and thus sales opportunities are affected. In low market cycle periods, marketing tactics can go into overdrive. What that means is your competitors will employ aggressive sales tactics to uncover any potential business opportunities. Changing product or service offerings could send the wrong signal to all your advocates. Instead, during low business cycles, entrepreneurs should be in a high communication mode. It would be time to stay close to your advocates rather than thinking about changing directions for your business. That would mean communicating with your customers and network professionals.

Your goal now is to position yourself between your competitors and your customers, acting as a protective barrier. The purpose is to retain customers. That protective layer is the relationship that you developed with the client. That relationship and what the client sees in you are a significant part of your brand. So, if you are wondering what to do today, my answer is to connect with at least five of your network advocates or clients every week. That means communicate with them. Be a partner to them. Provide problem-solving services to them. Be as indispensable to them as can be achieved. Regardless of the reasons for wanting to change the product or service mix early in the launch, patience may be a better alternative than altering your original market footprint. This is why there is a need for a measuring technique that can accurately assess market conditions.. In other words, you do not want to make changes based on inaccurate information. The research protocol and network relationships will help address this situation.

Another strategy to demonstrate patience is to run a simulation. This process tracks the expanded business idea in the marketplace, and projections are made to determine whether your initial thoughts were accurate. After a quarter or two of performance, you would begin to evaluate whether the option would have been beneficial or not to the business. If it had been useful, exploring how the change would affect current operations would have provided helpful information. You may move forward with the new line of business. If it was not beneficial, no investment was made to affect the business. No harm done.

I have described the decisions that entrepreneurs face when launching a business. I have provided some ideas that may help control the decision to expand. I have offered patience as a tool to create a mechanism to analyze carefully what information is driving this anxiety to expand early in the lifecycle of the business.

Perhaps understanding more about expansion anxiety and strategies to eliminate its presence may have great value to the entrepreneur. Let's explore expansion anxiety

EXPANSION ANXIETY

This represents a time when it's clear that the business is established and has a customer base to work with. Based on your work and connections with other businesses, you have identified additional marketing ideas that expand product and service offerings in different markets. If you now decide to change your product or service mix shortly after launching your business, what happens to your advocates? How will they feel when it's discovered that your brand has changed? What about those conversations they may have had with potential referrals that are expecting that image of you to appear to them precisely as it's been conveyed by your advocates? These questions and circumstances lead to a condition called expansion anxiety.

Expansion anxiety is closely tied to the vision you have for your business. If you see your business model as one that sells the business shortly after establishing the brand, then time is of the essence to grow quickly. Do whatever you need to do to get to the point where the brand fits neatly into the product line of another company. If you plan to hold the business and operate it over your lifetime, the mindset there would be to take your time and build it up over time. What if you decided to expand the business? What if there is undeniable evidence that there are opportunities out there that complement your current footprint? So if you do decide to expand, how do you go about expanding your business without harming your current brand platform? This is the dilemma that many entrepreneurs face in the early stages of their business development. So, how should you proceed? How do you manage this behavior?

Your anxiety about growing quickly may be eliminated through a carefully written mission statement. So, how does that work into the business plan? How can expansion anxiety be eliminated? How can I mitigate the risk of damaging the current branding platform with this new marketing direction?

There are two major ways to eliminate expansion anxiety that help to integrate new ideas into an existing company image. In other words, incorporating language into your business model can help eliminate the fear of harming your brand and reduce brand anxiety. Let's take a look.

EXPANSION STRATEGIES

Innovation

Innovation is a term commonly used to describe the process of discovery and improvement in a product or service. The word is utilized in many ways. Its primary use is to describe personnel or company structures that generate new ideas or processes. In other words, the company is innovative. So what does innovation have to do with shaping or reconfiguring branding platforms?

The word "innovation" has been utilized by many companies to describe themselves as being research-minded. It can also be used to denote that the company is a risk-taker in its industry. However it is defined, its purpose is to help companies enter different markets without harming its brand platform. This is especially true when the word innovation is part of the mission statement. It is also relevant when entrepreneurs utilize it in their elevator speeches. It could also be used to convey to customers how innovation is part of your brand. It's part of what the company delivers to customers.

An example of how innovation might play out for a company would be through the identification of customized markets. In other words, introducing more applications for your product or service mix would open up different market segments for the company. Here is an example of a statement that would address this concept:

ABC is a company that utilizes innovative processes to generate products and services that fit customized markets.

That last statement would allow you to produce just about anything and stay within your brand platform. The idea is that your business communities, along with customers, are not confused or bewildered by the changes in your product or service mix. The customers and network partners expect those processes to occur. Why? It's because you advertised yourself as an innovator, not simply a business owner.

Technology

Another strategy that helps companies change directions early in their development is the use of technology. Everyone who works anywhere understands the impact that technology has on companies. The changes that take place in both product and service mix are apparent across all organizations, both profit and non-profit. How can companies with a limited history transition into new markets without compromising their brand appeal? The use of technology may be the answer. Either it is utilized by itself, or in unison with innovation.

Let's examine how technology can be utilized to protect a company's brand platform. Providing guidance to your network and customer base is essential for it to be effective. Here is a statement that could cover it all:

Through the use of technology, XYZ offers state-of-the-art product development and service platforms that address multiple areas of interest in manufacturing and product design and development.

With such a statement, a company could start out producing any product and expand to others at any time. The explanation to the community for such moves would be reinforced in your elevator speech. New technologies could be expected, given that it's now part of your brand.

For an example of a company that has expanded its brand platform over the years, look to 3M Company.

3M Company

3M is a company that started mining mineral deposits to produce abrasives. The company's first successful product was sandpaper. Since 1902, the company has consistently added brands to its product line-up that go beyond its original name. 3M used to stand for Minnesota Mining and Manufacturing, but has since been officially named The 3M Company. When you examine its current product line-up and the number of brands it offers to the business and retail markets, it's mind-boggling. The different fields of interest included in the list of brands are impressive. A brief list of categories covered through 3M's branding platform is as follows: abrasives, adhesives, automotive parts, building materials, cleaning supplies, coatings and compounds, dental supplies, office supplies, and so much more. Every one of those categories of products has a brand attached to it. But it's the original brand that continues to speak to the buying community. How did the company manage to expand its product range to over 60,000 items while still maintaining the brand appeal of its original name? Well, through the mission statement, of course. The mission statement is simple. 3M utilized the words "science-based" to describe the products and services provided to its customers. Using a science-type strategy allowed for the use of innovation and technology to expand the original branding platform without confusing the customer base.

Thinking ahead to what your brand's footprint will look like requires a lot of foresight. I doubt that 3M Company had all of that product development in mind upfront as they launched the business from Two Harbors, Minnesota, in 1902. It does provide an example of how a company can expand into vastly different markets using a strategy that allows for an expansion of product offerings.

So far, we have had a lot of fun. Thinking about the launch, re-visiting the marketing plan often, and understanding the product line and service mix are all considered to be the soft part of the journey. You might think I have lost my mind saying it. There was nothing soft about it! The difference between Part I–IV and Part V is like day and night. Part V material has nothing to do with that passion you have developed for the business idea. It has nothing to do with the brand you have created or the product or service mix you have put together to launch as a business.

We will now shift gears significantly and move into Part V, which marks a major milestone in our journey into the administrative aspects of starting a business. Others refer to it as the hard side of the business. It gets its name from the idea that numerous rule structures are embedded into the material, making it more rudimentary and sterile than what was previously experienced. Part V will also introduce you to avoidance behavior. Part V is called The Aftermath because it is experienced after the launch of the business.

Takeaways from Part IV

- Establishing yourself in the community and marketplace is the beginning of the branding process
- Social media and website communication pieces are integral parts of your branding apparatus
- Symbols are the first impression people have of you as a brand

- Networking takes place through the entrepreneur's efforts and through the actions of advocates. Branding is formulated from both spheres of influence
- Brand longevity is a key attribute in the survivability of your business
- Early brand expansion can be detrimental to the overall branding process.
- Patience can be a tool that helps avoid premature branding expansions
- Expansion anxiety is a behavior that occurs when early success drives the motivation to pursue other product and service options.
- Innovation and technology can be utilized as concepts in the mission statement to reduce expansion anxiety

V

THE AFTERMATH

I t should be clear to you now that becoming an entrepreneur has many challenges that are rarely discovered in the dream state. Perhaps it's because our perceived reality prefers to be shaped into a utopian world where there are no challenges. Regardless, the reality comes into focus when the work to make a launch takes place. Piece by piece, the picture of what it's like to be an entrepreneur is made into a portrait of you. It is especially designed for you. In other words, not every entrepreneur becomes one in the same way. Nor do all individuals come to the role of entrepreneur through the same pathway.

There is one commonality, though, that does exist among entrepreneurs. That commonality exists when entrepreneurs are working to construct their business plans. Within the operations plan, there are those task structures that are common to operating a business. Regardless of the business you are involved in, these task structures remain universal. And for many, the challenge of remaining in business is often determined by the entrepreneur's ability to manage these task structures.

Unfortunately, there are gaps in the operations plan that fail to address the business in action. As the business is formulated and implemented, everything that is said is merely an image of what is thought to be necessary to operate the business. It's easy to talk about those operations from a distance. From a particular perspective, the business plan outlined the vision for how the business would operate. After the launch of the business, the words are replaced with experience. Those two worlds are not always precisely the same. This is where gaps are identified, which often result in additional costs for the entrepreneur. There can also be gaps in the company's research, which can alter the feasibility analysis. The market capitalization concept comes to mind. Is the market as big as what was projected in the pro-forma statements? Those are statements that project the assumption and projections about future events. The main event here is revenue generation. What if the actual activity is different than what was projected? With less revenue, how do the bills get paid? Is there a backup resource to tap in case this situation should happen? With more income than what was projected, how should those additional funds be allocated? These are a few questions that would need to be addressed.

In addition, as the business generates revenue, the terms used to describe its operations evolve into necessary task structures. For example, actions that require attention to revenue generation become essential to satisfy tax and legal regulations. For analysis and evaluation purposes, a system of operations must be maintained to determine what is needed in the business to maintain its viability. The reality is no longer perceived. The words are no longer simply words. It's time to operationalize the functions of the business to meet the demands created by the generation of revenue. Here are a few questions that would be pertinent to the Aftermath:

- How many employees do you need to hire?
- What would their job functions be?
- Who will answer the phone?
- How will product and service inquiries be handled?
- How do you order supplies?
- How much space is needed to operate?
- Who will manage the website
- Was anything not addressed in the original operational plan?

To gain a clearer understanding of what I am referring to, a tour of the landscape may help identify what deserves the entrepreneur's attention. I will also share with you a behavior present in the aftermath that can significantly impact the life and health of the business. This behavior is called avoidance behavior. We will explore the various areas within a business and demonstrate how those challenges can affect the entrepreneur's behavior. Let's begin our journey by working through the organizational plan.

THE ORGANIZATIONAL PLAN

When deciding on an organizational structure, a discussion about the various types of ownership available to prospective entrepreneurs should have taken place. For example, will the organization be operating as a sole proprietor? LLC? C-Corp? S-Corp? Partnership? Although it is not the purpose of this book to explore all of those options in detail, it is a point in the discussion of what actions are necessary after the decision is made. Whatever option was chosen, a protocol of actions must be maintained to meet the requirements of maintaining a business presence. Let's discuss those actions in detail for the group of organizational options as an aggregate.

The Protocol of the Organizational Plan

No matter which structure was chosen, some actions need to be taken to support the idea that you are operating a business. For example, most of the organizational types that are created require documentation to be kept in a filing system. In many cases, the company profile has to be maintained with the secretary of state's office. Some forms require meetings to be held by directors or associates who were named in the opening documents. The corporate meetings, as they are called, are held to document the activities of the company and to give authority to officers to act and make decisions. Those minutes and supporting documents need to be held in a filing system that is easily accessible. Although you may be the only person in the company at the time of the launch, documenting operational directives remains necessary. An example of an operational directive is the authority to open bank accounts for the business. Another is the authority to sign checks for the company. These requirements can cause some discomfort for the entrepreneur in several ways. Some entrepreneurs do not think it is necessary to document anything. Their record-keeping function is nonexistent. They simply purchase everything they need for the business without documenting the authority to do so. There is also the disregard for complying with reporting requirements. This failure to report to the state can lead to a "not in good standing" determination. This can jeopardize the legitimacy of the company, leading to numerous problems with tax and banking functions.

LLCs are formed to reduce some of these requirements, which makes them a popular choice for upstarts. It is discovered that state requirements are still part of the reporting process. The only relief comes in documenting the authority that officers have in conducting business for the company.

There is also some relief when there is the presence of multiple owners.

Regardless, there is still a need to document the existence of the company. I have witnessed the discomfort that entrepreneurs exhibit over these responsibilities. The search for eliminating such requirements creates a pushback behavior that can lead to pure avoidance. This push back in responsibility as an owner of the business can also be the beginning of more behavior that refuses to comply with these basic requirements. In other words, the behavior tends to bleed over into other areas of the business that have similar requirements. So how does this happen?

I refer back to the idea that words are one thing, actions are yet another. Writing down how your business is going to be organized is the easy part. The tricky part comes when it's time to maintain that structure according to a set of rules that you do not create. I have spoken to some entrepreneurs who have described these duties as the feeling of needles continuously pricking them. And if you decide to hire someone to maintain this system of requirements and activities, be prepared for the associated expenses. The amount of that expense may evoke the same feeling as the needles. Administrative tasks, such as maintaining company and officer profiles with the secretary of state and keeping meeting minutes, are only one aspect of this duty. Let's venture into the banking world to examine another part of the picture.

BANKING

To secure the business's receipts, bank accounts are opened. Bank accounts are known as operational vehicles. They help operationalize the cash flow for the company. Many entrepreneurs would respond that it's no problem to open up bank accounts. Many people discount the process because they apply the knowledge they gained when opening their own accounts. After arriving at the bank, it will not take long to gain a different perspective. Business accounts are different than personal accounts. Opening a Business account requires that the documentation of the organizational structure be provided. For corporations, an 'articles of incorporation' document would be an example of what banks require. Another requirement is the minutes of a corporate meeting giving the authority to open bank accounts. Another requirement is the proof of the tax ID generated by the government. Entrepreneurs have expressed frustration with these requirements, as they believe it is unnecessary to provide all the documentation. This is especially true if you are the only person involved in the business so far. Because the accounts are being opened with a business tax ID, the bank will require documentation to prove that the business is registered and operating as a business. Entrepreneurs often make the mistake of pushing everything through their personal bank account, rather than navigating the hurdles of requirements. Or maybe they want to open business accounts but realize they haven't structured the business correctly. Frustration and anger from this problem can lead to avoidance behavior. Yet there are still other hurdles that need to be addressed to open a bank account for your business.

The cost of maintaining a business account is another factor that may influence the generation of avoidance behavior. Not only are the checking accounts more expensive to maintain, but other services may also add to the bottom line. Lines of credit come to mind. Establishing a line of credit at the bank is important in times when cash flow is not enough to cover expenses. Borrowing money to cover those expenses can be done through the bank. But at what interest rate? Depending on your credit history, you may get a reasonable interest rate.

On the other hand, you may be surprised at the interest rates for business-type transactions. And the amount of the loan available may also surprise you. Given your company's limited history, why would a bank lend you a substantial amount of money? Because of this reality, collateral may be necessary to secure a line of credit. When looking for collateral, some entrepreneurs will consider utilizing their retirement assets, as most people hold a majority of their assets in retirement accounts. Well, retirement assets cannot be used as collateral for a line of credit. Retirement assets are generally protected from the liens of creditors. This means that if the bank tried to assess the collateral to satisfy a loan payment, that collateral would not be accessible. Thus, it is worthless as a piece of collateral. So, establishing a sufficient line of credit to cover downturns in revenue flow may take some time to develop. Banks require income statements and balance sheets to support the ability to make the payments for such a loan. And those statements need to have numbers. Which means there needs to be some level of revenue generation.

You may have noticed that many of these requirements I have addressed are linked together. Many operational functions are linked together similarly. In this case, the first link was from the supporting documents for the organizational type. The second link was from the proof of the establishment of a tax ID. The third link was to have an accounting system that keeps track of the company's financial activities. The fourth link was to provide income statements and balance sheets as proof that the company's cash flow can support the size of the line of credit requested. All of these links are ingredients to the approval process for a line of credit. Without prior knowledge of such linked activities, it would be easy to miss one. your company would have a difficult time securing a line of credit.

On another front, when money cannot be obtained from banks, entrepreneurs will revert to using their own assets to meet the demand for money to operate their businesses. In a corporate entity, or any entity for that matter, this would not be a good strategy since the influx of money would be seen as a loan to the business. In corporate entities, authority to accept the money would need to be approved by the board. A document would need to be generated outlining the loan terms with an interest rate (imputed interest rate) attached to it. That is an IRS requirement that needs to be satisfied if the company later deducts the interest as an expense to the business. Any other arrangement that does not document the transaction is avoiding disclosure. The corporate bank account is not your piggy bank. Without disclosure, the transaction becomes income taxable to the entrepreneur. And by the way, the board may be just you, which seems silly to many who have experienced this situation. I can say with certainty that accountants would require that loan documentation be completed, no matter what structure is in place. So if you should hire one to help with your accounting functions, expect that type of logic to be offered. Entrepreneurs have responded to this situation by discounting the requirements and validating the idea that it's not necessary to comply with these banking requirements. They will deposit the money into their personal accounts and then transfer it to a business account once they can establish one. They may use personal credit cards to access cash instead of waiting to establish a line of credit. There are yet more problems with these arrangements.

One major problem arises when your company tries to collect payment for goods and services rendered. The problem here is that to conduct business, clients would have to make the payment for goods or services to you personally. Since you have no business account established, how else can you be paid? In cash? Good luck. Most companies may object to doing so. They prefer to write checks to company entities to avoid the possibility of it being treated as an employee transaction. If the check is made out to the business, it can only be deposited into a business account with the company's name on it. If the company makes the payment to you personally, the customer would have the concern that the payment may be misconstrued as a payroll check. Companies avoid writing checks directly to people due to the independent contractor rules outlined by the IRS. These rules determine whether someone is an employee or an independent contractor. In other words, the company does not want you to be looked at or mistakenly categorized as an employee. This mistake would trigger the inclusion in the benefits system. That would incur a cost that was unexpected for sure. (Are you dizzy yet?)

Another point to make here is that it has to do with the corporate veil. It's the protective seal that separates personal assets from corporate assets. It separates business behavior from personal behavior. If the company receipts are placed in the entrepreneur's name, the veil of the corporate structure will be broken. Now the veil of a business structure has also been broken. This can leave you vulnerable if a lawsuit should take place. When lawyers are looking for money to attach a claim to, they will identify what is accessible. If the lawyer can prove that there is a breach of that veil, personal accounts can be utilized to satisfy that claim. This is not a place you want to be. The separation between you and the business is an essential strategy for the sustainability of the business.

Rather than go to a bank or rely on your own assets, some entrepreneurs prefer to open a GoFundMe account or seek third-party funding such as venture capital. Although there is nothing wrong with this strategy, a protocol is attached to such funding options. Who is going to loan you money without some documentation of what the business is and how it operates? You will need to open the doors and allow outsiders to assess the company's ability to make payments. Is this company a vital business entity? Those embracing short-cut methods of operating will not have those guests for long. Would you invest in a project with little history and incomplete documentation for revenue generation? This outside funding idea may be more relevant when there is more business activity to support a loan situation.

The idea of separating assets, mentioned previously, can also be a critical element when someone wants to buy your business. Personal and business assets are not considered separate assets when determining the business's valuation. To recover your personal assets, you will need to make a transaction. That transaction is transparent. Buyers may start to ask questions about the operation of the business when the transaction is discovered. This can result in a significant dip in value or a cadre of questions as to the nature of the transaction.. So, the message here is, do not comingle personal assets with business assets! Stay away from avoidance behavior!

Entrepreneurs have had moments of frustration with this banking process, especially if they're the only employee in the organization. The separation of business from personal activities is a source of frustration. This is where that avoidance behavior starts to influence the actions of the entrepreneur. Some make the mistake of using a personal account to avoid such requirements. This is a critical mistake, as was discussed previously. Without a separation of the business from the person, tax deductions can be disallowed by the Internal Revenue Service. Purchasing office furniture and computers to create an office environment should be paid for from a business account. If a Section 179 tax deduction is taken for the purchase of those items on the company tax return, the Internal Revenue Service will want to know how those items were purchased. If from a personal account, why should a business deduction be allowed? For example, a Section 179 deduction allows for the full deduction of the cost of an asset in the year it was purchased. This is in contrast to having to depreciate the asset over many years. So it is a huge tax deduction for the business.

As you can see, avoidance behavior can get an entrepreneur in trouble quickly. And even if I assume that the entrepreneur was able to implement remedies to avoid the requirements successfully, there remains a question that many may ask. Are you operating a business or simply operating as a hobby? Is this a lifestyle business that will have little residual value when you retire? If a business does not operate like a business, should it be afforded all the privileges of a business? This is the overall question that the IRS will ask.

Another legal intervention that is necessary to account for is if your business enters into contracts. This is another example of where avoidance behavior lingers. Unless you have a background in contract law, it would be a good idea to have counsel when entering into a contract. Right? Yet this is another area where avoidance behavior takes over and becomes a rationale for interpreting the conditions of the contract without counsel. And given the fact that there are performance requirements in contracts, what performance requirements are you committing yourself to? Would it not be best to secure counsel to guide you through these contracts? Oh yes, it costs money. What would it cost if you misinterpreted the contract and were forced to comply with something that does not benefit your company? Avoiding the expense is not a viable option.

The following situation is also one that the entrepreneur often avoids. That situation would be the cost of insuring the business and the business environment. Whether it's officer liability insurance or comprehensive business insurance, the decision to embrace the concept requires a company to be established. Failing to insure means you leave your assets, business, and personal belongings vulnerable. Let's take a deeper dive into insurance.

INSURANCE

Insurance is one of those commodities in business that few people enjoy making premium payments for. It is a strategy to divert the liability of actions to someone other than yourself. It could very well be the last decision made in the start-up process. But when the liability question becomes more feasible as an occurrence, and there are now assets that can be lost to the process of a lawsuit, suddenly, there is a renewed interest in being insured. Some entrepreneurs consider the expense to be a waste of assets. The rationale that nothing is going to happen that would warrant a lawsuit begins to be a consideration in the decision process. Procrastination is the start of the avoidance behavior. "I will do that later". And like anything else, it becomes a forgotten thought that rarely comes up until the entrepreneur seeks to office somewhere. Or build a storefront, factory, or warehouse somewhere.

Now, the leasing company wants proof of insurance for the premises. It is common for this expense to be forgotten. To protect yourself, it's essential to have an insurance policy in place, as the office management may otherwise purchase one for you. If the policy is purchased for you, I am confident that you will not be pleased with the premium. Insurance is also applicable when you have a corporate board and officer positions. Officer and board member liability insurance would need to be purchased because few people will risk their own assets to be an officer or board member for your company. This is why it is an essential element of your operational plan.

Insuring the company's assets are another key aspect of your operational plan. Insurance companies want to know who they are insuring. Protection against fire and weather-related perils is essential to protect, perhaps, your inventory. Your inventory is needed to help serve customer needs and generate revenue. Losing it in a fire or weather-related event could be detrimental to the company's survivability. Like it or not, it's an expense of doing business. It is also a tentacle of common sense. If you owned the company asset instead of leasing one, could you afford to replace the asset with the current level of cash flow? Do you treat the house that you own in the same way? Allowing avoidance behavior to determine whether to insure or not can lead to excessive liability exposure. Now your company will operate as a high-risk entity. It simply is not a viable business option.

Our next topic within this administrative task heaven is the discussion about taxes. This includes all taxes the company is subject to paying. It also includes the recordkeeping needed to justify paying what is owed. Without support documentation, that tax issue will be another thorn in your side.

TAXES

Let's now examine the subject of taxation and what requirements it imposes on a company. Given the intensity of work necessary to file reports to the IRS, entrepreneurs struggle to meet these requirements. That struggle often leads to avoidance behavior.

When someone refers to the subject of taxation, it often gets an adverse reaction from the masses. I know few people who actually like paying taxes. Entrepreneurs are no different. But the reasons for their response have to do with the added documentation necessary to support expense deductions, among other things. It's important to make the distinction to visualize what needs to be addressed to stay compliant. In addition, understanding the impact of taxation issues on entrepreneurs will reveal another reason why the situation fosters avoidance behavior.

TAXATION ISSUES

Many entrepreneurs are considered to be self-employed. This also applies to those who decided to incorporate. Some would argue that claim. The corporation pays a share of the payroll taxes for the employee, so how is that considered being self-employed? The reason is simple. Who is the company, and who is the employee? Are they the same? Here is a key point I am trying to make. When entrepreneurs become employees in their own firms, the corporation pays one-half of the social security for each employee. If the employee is the owner, where does the money come from to pay the Social Security taxes? It comes from the generation of revenue. Who generates the revenue? In a small start-up, it's the entrepreneur who started the company. Given the case, both sides of the social security funding platform are paid for from the entrepreneurs' efforts. The same holds in a non-corporate structure, such as a sole proprietor. The sole proprietorship situation is often referred to as being self-employed. And because of this status, both sides of the social security funding platform are paid by the entrepreneur. Small corporate structures can be looked at in the same way. Although I am sure I would get some pushback from the accounting community regarding that comment.

Given all of that, self-employed individuals are required to pay quarterly estimated tax payments to the government. Corporations generally make payments more often than they deduct from an employee's paycheck. That means self-employed people need to know how much to send. That means there needs to be a system to keep track of revenue and expenses. Income must be determined to send an estimated amount within the penalty boundaries. Penalties are assessed if the estimated income is significantly lower than the actual taxable income for the period. Bottom line, it means that a self-employed person is responsible for declaring estimated income. Often, the IRS will look back at the amount paid on last year's tax return to assess whether there is an underpayment situation. So there is some guesswork here that can cause some discomfort. Consider when the entrepreneur was a corporate employee, before starting the business. Taxes were taken from each paycheck, and the employer passed them along to the government. As an employee, you paid half of the Social Security amounts. The employer paid the other half. Digging deeper into the social security scenario, the self-employed person pays 15.3% instead of the 7.65% paid when they worked for someone else. The other 7.65% was paid as a benefit to the employee (you). It was part of the compensation system. For self-employed individuals, there is some relief in reducing the adjusted gross income by one-half of the self-employment tax paid on the tax return. (Thank you, Uncle Sam.)

Employees are often unaware of this situation until it affects them. When starting a business, it will be front and center when calculating tax liabilities. The process alone can affect them. The process adds to the workload of the entrepreneur, affecting their overall performance. So when it is unveiled to them as new owners of a company, the reaction is often one of disbelief. Surely it is a candidate to influence avoidance behavior. And if funds are tight, this payroll/tax function can go adrift. It is a federal offense not to submit payroll taxes for those who work for you. So, often a payroll service is hired to take care of all of it. As long as the money is there, it may not be a bad idea.

Many beginning entrepreneurs believe they can rely on an accountant to handle all their tax work. The reality is, most start-ups cannot afford a full-time accountant to do this work. The entrepreneur is responsible for gathering all the necessary data to present to the accountant they hire to file their taxes. That remedy is common. It is especially common as well if the company is required to collect sales taxes on sales receipts. The problem that arises here is that payroll taxes and sales taxes are sensitive requirements. If the payroll/sales tax function runs adrift, there could be legal action taken against you for not filing. The reason? Technically, it's not your money. The payroll taxes belong to the employee, which eventually is credited toward taxes owed by the employee to the government. The sales taxes belong to the state, and they will not be happy if those receipts are not paid on time. So it is illegal to retain these monies for your own purpose past the reporting date. And yes, there is such a thing as jail time for tax fraud. You cannot afford to avoid the required tax reporting functions.

And all of this work to pay taxes has nothing to do with the marketing of the firm. Gathering the necessary information, determining what to submit to the government, learning how to complete the forms, and ensuring the money is available to pay the tax bill all require time. And that cycle is continuous. When do I network? When do I market? Welcome to the world of owning a business. Perhaps the comments I made earlier in the book about walking into the abyss are appropriate, given the complexity of this situation.

There is another way to address this issue that many entrepreneurs consider a reasonable strategy to avoid all of this self-employment taxation garbage. If you are the only employee of the company, you may decide not to pay yourself for a while. By exercising avoidance behavior, entrepreneurs have essentially created a source of income for themselves. Through a concept called "return of capital." This would be money that was placed in the business from personal accounts that can now be removed as capital. It is not subject to taxes or social security. Since many entrepreneurs invest their own capital in the business, it makes sense to get it out without taxation. But that would be the limit of it. And why would that be the case? Plain and simple. If social security is not paid in on your work record, your social security payments at retirement would be much less than if the taxes were paid according to the schedule laid out by the government. Many entrepreneurs who have chosen this route of avoidance wake up when they finally want to retire. Considering the amounts they would receive from Social Security, they may regret not paying the taxes back when the decision to take a return on capital was made. It will also affect the asking price when you decide to sell the business and retire. You will need a higher asking price to compensate for the benefits you are not receiving from Social Security. This certainly places additional stress on the situation.

Another part of the taxation issue that is different for business owners is the requirement to file an income tax return. Although almost everyone has the experience of filing an income tax return, things change a bit when you become an owner of a business. Even sole proprietors file additional forms. For example, a Schedule C is used to report revenue and expenses for the business. That form is then attached to the Form 1040. Corporate entities, though, file separate tax returns and are taxed based on a different tax schedule. This requirement adds to the workload of the entrepreneur. It also requires that income statements and balance sheets be maintained. And like the other activities that need to be kept for corporations (e.g., minutes to meetings), the additional activities begin to create a workload that can again interfere with the generation of revenue. The pressure of these requirements also influences the search for alternatives. Another alternative is not to hire employees at all. The avoidance behavior again becomes a go-to strategy to find another method that avoids what is not comfortable or affordable. As you can see, as avoidance behavior starts to be generated from the various functions of the organization, the results begin to dampen the viability of the business. One additional function that adds to this avoidance is the establishment and maintenance of a benefits plan for employees.

BENEFITS ADMINISTRATION

Every business organization deals with the issue of providing benefits to its employees. When entrepreneurs step into the abyss, surely the decision about their own health care has to be made. After leaving a company and starting a business, some entrepreneurs use COBRA rules to extend their health insurance. This insurance is offered as a way to eliminate gaps in health care coverage. These policies can be expensive. Polices based on self-employment can even be more expensive. Many entrepreneurs find they cannot afford to purchase a policy like the one they had with their previous employer. As you add employees, the bill becomes a significant additional expense beyond the salaries paid. Entrepreneurs avoid this issue by either going uninsured or taking out a high-deductible policy. Some have considered health savings plans. What they discover is that those plans are not exactly a bargain. As the entrepreneur feels as though they are backed into a corner, avoidance behavior begins to creep into the decision-making process. I have witnessed owners attempting to hire people under a compensation system that offers no benefits. Some try to hire strictly independent contractors to come and perform the labor. Given the competition for qualified labor, who is going to consider taking a job without benefits? And given that the independent contractor rule is one that government agencies do investigate, this could be something that comes back to bite you.

Here is an example. Say you have five independent contractors working for you. You pay them a high hourly rate to lure them to your firm. Since you pay no benefits, the hourly wage is often higher to compensate for this. As independent contractors, they are responsible for handling their own estimated tax payments to the government. In other words, they are looked at like self-employed individuals, even though they only work for you. Let's say one of those five fails to pay estimated taxes to the government. If the independent contractor fails to submit an estimated tax payment, there could be an issue with the employee's status. Are they an employee or an independent contractor? It could also be discovered through a forensic analysis of the 1099 generated by the company for the employee. If the only source of income is from one company, how can they be considered self-employed?

Bingo. The 20-point rule for classifying whether an individual is an independent contractor or not will be applied. If it is determined that the person was actually treated like an employee, you will face a situation you do not want to experience. Part of that analysis will include whether or not taxes were submitted for the independent contractor. If it is discovered that there were payments made, then where is the proof? If the entrepreneur considers having independent contractors work for them and deducts payroll taxes, the independent contractor rules are now broken. In other words, the independent contractor is automatically considered an employee because they are treated as one. Lawsuits, penalties, and aggravation could be coming your way. Are you willing to take the chance? I will let you ponder that question on your own.

There are other examples of avoidance behavior where the entrepreneur decides to drop coverage and wing it. Raising the salary of everyone in the company becomes a strategy to avoid offering health insurance to them. The logic here is that employees can use the extra income to purchase an individual health care plan. Periodic visits to the doctor can be paid for with the additional salary paid for that purpose. The logic here is that by paying cash, an individual can negotiate health care fees and reduce the cost of doctor visits and simple office procedures. For surgery and hospital visits, though, that strategy is very limited. Given that it is limited, it still does not address the considerable cost of hospital visits and surgical procedures. A hospital visit alone could wipe out a person's entire estate. Are you willing to take that risk? And employees usually try to get coverage anyway because they recognize this liability. By paying the premiums from their take-home pay, the competitiveness of the compensation system is reduced considerably. Good luck getting qualified employees to work for you.

Another key benefit of the plan is whether it will offer retirement benefits to employees. Although some options are more cost-effective than others, every move has an impact on what the entrepreneur can accomplish as a highly-paid individual. This status as a highly-paid individual is a term used in the rules covering ERISA. Let's take a look at what retirement benefits look like.

RETIREMENT BENEFITS

Entrepreneurs rarely embrace programs that provide retirement benefits. The bottom line is that they simply do not have the cash flow early on to give themselves a retirement program. This is another element that drives entrepreneurs into avoidance behavior. The thinking, as I have witnessed it, is that a retirement program will be started when the business grows more. Many entrepreneurs never get there. The needs of the company early on force entrepreneurs to reinvest money back into the company. This leaves little money for retirement contributions. As the company grows, it may face the challenge of allocating profits to projects that expand the company's footprint in the market. Salaries may have been low for the entrepreneur early on, which would leave little money for home repairs, car repairs, and many other typical household and personal expenses. Now it's time to replenish the household, which leaves little for retirement. Another simpler reason is that entrepreneurs do not want to pay more for the cost of an employee retirement plan. Remember the idea I mentioned before about cost? It's the cost of doing business. Yet, I have witnessed instances where this idea seems to be the last item on the company's to-do list.

Many entrepreneurs believe that they can sell the business down the road. This then could be their retirement plan, along with Social Security. I do understand this logic. But some cautionary ideas should be considered. A business is not set up to sell when it is based only on the entrepreneur's efforts in generating income. The sale may result in a small amount of money, as the sales revenue may be difficult to transfer to someone else. And applying all that has been cited about those activities that are the result of avoidance behavior, there would be a high probability that the business would yield little, too. Why? By avoiding the need to secure a tax ID, eliminating the need for employees, and operating on a least-cost basis, what is there for someone to buy? Without you, there is no business. Some buyers may pay for your client list. Some buyers will pay for residual income generated from the business that the buyer can assume. And if the entrepreneur operated based on paying themselves through a return-on-capital process instead of a salary, the amount of social security they could expect may be disappointing. As a reminder, the return-on-capital process is essentially a substitute for salary, designed to avoid paying self-employment tax and social security payments. This places pressure on the sales price. It also influences the number of potential buyers interested in purchasing it.

Now, let's assume that employees are hired. When companies grow and hire employees, retirement benefits become an important issue to consider. Because of the rules surrounding retirement plans, owners generally are not allowed to contribute outside of a calculated percentage of their income. These rules are encased within the ERISA (Employee Retirement Income Security Act). The frustration of incurring the expense to maintain a plan for all employees without a sizeable reward to the entrepreneur is yet another hurdle that entrepreneurs have to resolve. The higher expense plans for retirement (e.g., 401(k)) can create a sizable reward to the entrepreneur. But it comes at a higher cost to the company. Believe it or not, some entrepreneurs become so upset over this situation that they prefer to invest in Roth IRAs as a strategy to fund retirement. This strategy would leave employees out in the cold. The only problem with that strategy is that it is means-tested. This means that high-salaried individuals are not eligible to participate in the program. Since the owner would probably be making a high salary at some point, this would eliminate the option of a Roth IRA. As I've been told time and again throughout my business career, it's the cost of doing business. Yeah. I feel better already.

Entrepreneurs could decide to offer low-cost plans. Corporate individual retirement accounts or SIMPLE plans have little administrative cost to the company. But because of ERISA rules, the plans cannot discriminate. That means everyone else receives the same benefits in the plan, and the same rules apply to the entrepreneur. This is what was meant earlier about offering plans that do not effectively benefit the entrepreneur, even though the entrepreneur is paying for the program. Ouch.

There are yet other options that would include a company profit-sharing program. Entrepreneurs can gain favor through these programs. They gain favor because the methodology to determine the payout amount is based on an employee's income. Highly-paid employees would then receive a higher amount of money. However, there is also an obligation to pay your employees, as your company cannot discriminate.

Remember the ERISA rules? If it is determined that your company's retirement program is discriminatory, all contributions to the plan could now become taxable. I have only witnessed this once in my career. It was a mess. Employers will take all necessary steps to prevent the termination of their retirement plan.

There are many sophisticated retirement strategies that I have not talked about here because, frankly, many are not relevant to those entrepreneurs who have just launched their businesses. Those strategies will come to the surface in their own time. This especially applies when there is enough money to plan a catch-up strategy. These are strategies that have a high contribution limit.

One last area that needs to be addressed is the regulatory and legal issues that companies face. Some of the major ones generally apply to employee benefit programs

Regulatory and Legal Issues.

Taxation, payroll, health care, and retirement activities change all the time. Keeping up with those changes can be challenging by itself. Claiming not to be aware of the changes is not acceptable to the government. As a business owner, it is your responsibility to know. With the euphoria of owning your own business comes the reality of what it actually means. Those who welcome the challenge and work through the challenges will find it to be an exhilarating experience. The pride of the accomplishment never gets old.

Every year, there are changes in the employee benefits programs that have to be reflected in the program you are operating. Tax rates change. This means that payroll systems have to be adjusted accordingly. The amount employees can contribute to their retirement plans changes every year, too. New maximums have been announced and need to be conveyed to your employees. Compliance requirements may be adjusted periodically to reflect someone's vision for effectiveness. Regulations concerning safety can affect job descriptions and required employee conduct. Health care premiums change every year to reflect changes in incidence rates and inflation. Changes in the number of employees within your company can usher in additional regulatory requirements. This typically begins to occur when your company reaches fifteen or more employees.

I have already touched on the contract issue that requires counsel to interpret and provide guidance. Certainly, as your company grows, there is a need for counsel for employee grievances and lawsuits that may be generated from claims of mismanagement. Consumers could generate legal work by suing your company. This can happen when consumers are injured by using your product. Because you are vulnerable to lawsuits, legal counsel will have to be retained to protect you and your company from predators. The recent identity theft occurring within companies, along with cybercrime, is definitely a liability worth addressing as well.

Many issues arise, but listing them all is too voluminous. The point here is that the regulatory and legal component of your operations plan is ongoing. It requires effort to manage it. That effort comes from you.

Moving on to another task structure that needs your attention is the purchase of the physical items, like furniture, computers, and décor.

PHYSICAL START-UP COSTS

In the process of thinking about your business in the dream state, the complete picture of the business is rarely clear. In developing a business plan, the actual start-up costs can be different than what was projected. If good research was conducted, your numbers may be very accurate. But what if your numbers are inaccurate? In my experience, this is an area that often gets overlooked. Estimates are given based on holistic situations. In other words, there are no specific layouts with dimensions that determine precisely what is needed for operations. Entrepreneurs who lease office space often encounter this cost issue. Those who have a storefront business or factory facility are less prone to guessing what is needed to operate the business. The avoidance behavior arises from the illusion that I can just work from home and save money. This applies to those who will utilize an office to operate the business. It does not apply to storefront or factory-type scenarios. Going back to Part IV, remember the launch process. Remember how important it was to establish your brand. Can you imagine trying to establish yourself by operating the business from an extra bedroom? Yet so many entrepreneurs do this with the idea of getting an office in the future after the business grows. They fail to connect the image with the brand concept, which is why the failure rate for entrepreneurship is so high.

Some reminders that have been shared earlier are to purchase the physical items with business income or business credit. (Nothing personal.) One strategy that has been rationalized is to lease furniture. Another is to purchase discount furniture, which is pre-owned. Neither one of these strategies is wrong. It is an example of how to transform avoidance behavior into something credible. It is a solution that aligns with the operational plans' objectives but requires less capital in the company's early stages. Probably a smart move, provided the furniture meets the requirements of the image projected for the company.

From this perspective, then, it should be clear that the fundamentals in creating and documenting your business idea are important steps that have long-lasting effects on everything that will come after the launch. Operational objectives are just as important to the business as marketing strategies, including branding and networking. It is my opinion that avoidance behavior can affect even the best of us if we allow ourselves to be driven by it. Avoidance behavior is a phenomenon that can alter the course of your efforts to start and maintain a business. Through the examples I have given, I believe I have made it clear that avoidance behavior is not your friend. Avoidance behavior is like a snowball rolling down a hill. The snowball gets larger and larger as it descends. The more you utilize strategies that are produced through avoidance behavior, the greater will be its influence on the operation of the company. As avoidance behavior expands to other task structures, the business becomes increasingly weaker and unsustainable as a viable entity. And eventually, there is little value that exists to sell. It can limit the potential of your ideas in creating something like the Mona Lisa.

LET'S FLIP THE COIN

The Aftermath section of this book discusses numerous administrative functions that often bother beginning entrepreneurs. Identifying them and discussing why they are troublesome is part of my strategy to inform you. You now know what those difficult areas are and perhaps how to make sure they are included in your operations plan. The administrative functions do not have to be painful. All can be handled with careful planning. And although many of these areas may not be part of your expertise now, over time and with repeated effort, you can begin to link together how all of these functions should operate. That does not mean you will do all the work. It means you understand how the work fits into the bigger picture. You are a manager, not a task structure journeyman. Overseeing and managing operations is an effective way to build a sustainable business. Although the Aftermath may take some time to understand, it is not intended to be a short-term learning episode. Part V: The Aftermath has no termination date; it is ongoing. Like everything in this book, it is a life experience. Building it is like building a house. Your foundation must be strong and sturdy to be able to add floors of opportunities onto it. Mistakes along the way can happen. Knowing why they are mistakes and laying out a plan to fix them is like reshaping a piece of clay. It can be handled. It can be re-shaped to reflect the new knowledge that has been incorporated in finding the discrepancy. With all that said, let's move to our conclusion of this magnificent journey.

Takeaways from Part V:

- All entrepreneurs, regardless of their type of business, have a common challenge in operating their businesses: The operating plan
- Administrative task structures have just as much importance as marketing to the operation of a business
- All organizational types have documentation requirements that require the attention of the entrepreneur.
- Corporate entities have the highest level of documentation needed to operate
- When establishing bank accounts, separate business affairs from personal ones
- Operating like a business requires levels of activity called linked activities. Those linkages generate programs that help operationalize the business
- Ensuring your business and its operations are protected protects the efforts made to produce an effective launch
- Tax issues range from payroll to income liability. Understanding how taxes operate helps to alleviate costly decision-making

- Employee benefit programs require an understanding to address the legal requirements necessary for their survival
- Physical start-up costs require the entrepreneur to accurately account for office, storefront, and warehouse/factory physical layouts, along with the décor that matches the image of the company's branding strategy
- Understanding the Aftermath helps to build a more effective operations plan within the business plan

CONCLUSION

In writing this book, I have had the opportunity to share with you the reader the many behaviors I have witnessed over the last thirty-four years as a wealth manager. I also worked as a consultant in the outplacement industry, counseling people who had lost their jobs. As a small business consultant, I gained extensive experience discussing potential entrepreneurs' ideas and aspirations for starting a business. As a professor for the last forty-two years, I have taught the subject of entrepreneurship in corporate and academic environments. From all of this experience, I thought it was about time to get all of this information under one roof, this book.

For me, it's always been a way of life, not a job choice. As an entrepreneur, I never felt like I was going to work. I did not punch a time clock. I organized my life to include everything that came my way. I wanted to be an entrepreneur. I wanted to be the owner. If you would consider that same perspective for yourself, you may find that the money and material aspects of owning your own business will subside. It will become a spiritual experience that has no boundaries. The independence and freedom that come with owning your own business can help eliminate obstacles to your success. The challenges you face will be reduced to a moment in time. It surely will cease to be an event that acts like a fork-in-the-road moment. Those challenges will be welcomed as opportunities for learning and growth in the business, rather than roadblocks and setbacks. And the change-over in experience from day-to-day will provide more perspective on what is really important to you. And know you have a vehicle to get there. You have broken the seal that secured all of your possibilities as an employee. The world is available to you now. In everyday life, the next dream state emerges, one that is looking to be realized. The storylines will continue to appear. You will recognize its message more clearly now. You will venture through them as if journeying to the next sphere of consciousness. It's all available for you

Personal note

This book itself can help assess whether there is logic in your choice of becoming self-employed. Perhaps it can serve as a guide for what to expect from your new endeavor. The feasibility of your business idea may be better realized through some of the suggestions in this book. However, it may help you. I hope the book serves as a resource for beginning entrepreneurs, helping them make their launch more successful. For entrepreneurs who have been around for a while, this may help explain a few things, leading to a better understanding of their circumstances.

And for those of you wondering where this idea came from to write this book, it's an easy answer. I have been dreaming of this book for many years. I dreamt about what I would write about. I thought about how I would lay out the book. I finally decided to launch my book-writing project. As you can see, I am very experienced with the dream state. Sharing that with you was more than just a story. It was a piece of my experience as one who has dreamt about many endeavors in my life.

And those dreams will not stop. But this book I consider to be my launch as a writer. I will have to wait for the next cue before writing anything else. As I see it now, no matter how my community receives the book, I am blessed to have had the opportunity to express myself. It has been a behavioral journey in writing this book. There were many moments of deep reflection on the experiences I have had over a forty-two-year period. And now in my dream state, I can see more is to come that may be worth writing about.

I want to thank my wife, Sujuan, for putting up with me over these many months. Getting up in the middle of the night and writing about my visions that came during the night also affected her. Her support and the support of my children have also been a joy to experience. I appreciate all of my colleagues and friends who have encouraged me to write the book. I especially want to thank Jenny Wang for her assistance in getting the book process started for me.

ABOUT THE AUTHOR

Dale G. Konicek, Ph.D., is a serial entrepreneur who has invested time in observing the behavior of those seeking to become entrepreneurs. His self-employment experience started in 1961 as a paperboy for the *Cleveland Plain Dealer*. Early on, Dr. Konicek recognized the opportunity to serve the needs of people. Throughout his teenage years, he worked in service-oriented occupations that sparked his interest in studying customer behavior.

After completing high school, he started a construction and landscaping business that flourished over the years. Working in factories and warehouses as a laborer, alongside his landscaping business, he decided that a college education was necessary to further grow in his pursuits.

After graduating with a BBA from Kent State University in 1981, the job market in Cleveland was such that he decided to pursue a career elsewhere. Dr. Konicek relocated to Houston, Texas, in 1982. He worked for Houston Lighting and Power as an analyst and later as a consultant. During that time, Dr. Konicek pursued a second job teaching at Houston Community College. In 1983, he became an adjunct instructor in the Marketing and Management division. In 1985, he was hired full-time with the College. Shortly thereafter, he pursued an MBA from the University of Houston-Clear Lake. He graduated with an MBA in 1986. Afterward, he attended Texas A&M

University in pursuit of a Ph.D. He graduated with his Ph.D. in 1990. After returning to Houston Community College, Dr. Konicek transitioned to the University of Houston in 1991. There, he began working with industry partners on projects focused on quality improvement and executive management development. Dr. Konicek started his own business in 1992 as a consultant and later expanded his business to include wealth management services. As a wealth manager, Dr. Konicek was a top producer for many years until his retirement in 2024.

From an academic and industrial perspective, Dr. Konicek has taught the subject of entrepreneurship to those seeking knowledge about starting a business. He conducted numerous entrepreneurship seminars in industry through an outplacement company. He has also taught entrepreneurship classes at Houston Community College. He has also volunteered to work as a Mentor with the Center for Entrepreneurship at Houston Community College.

Dr. Konicek has also been involved with community activities throughout his career. Some major affiliations are as follows: The Katy Chamber of Commerce (board member, president), the West Houston Chamber of Commerce (committee chair), The West Houston Leadership Institute, Houston Community College Business Management Advisory Board (chair), The Houston Ballet Foundation (trustee), and the Calvin Nelms Charter School Board of Directors (currently president).

In addition to community activities, Dr. Konicek has funded three endowments supporting faculty development at Texas A&M University and Kent State University. Dr. Konicek and his wife, Sujuan, recently participated in funding the Ambassador Crawford School of Business and Entrepreneurship program at Kent State University.

Dr. Konicek is currently employed full-time at Houston City College as a faculty member.